GOD'S UGLY

PASTOR LERONE DINNALL

ISBN 978-1-957956-72-5 (Paperback)
ISBN 978-1-957956-73-2 (Ebook)

Inquiries and Book Orders should be addressed to:

Leavitt Peak Press
17901 Pioneer Blvd Ste L #298, Artesia, California 90701
Phone #: 2092191548

CONTENTS

TARGETS...

Everything has a link, whether Spiritual or Physical the connection is there. For everything there must be the maintenance to sustain the life of its existence, whenever production to sustain for maintenance is affected we know that the life span is cut shorter than the time it is expected to last. We know that the laws of that which we can understand manifest that if there is no floor to step then no physical steps can be made for the person who desires to make one step. We know that once an overload of pressure is applied to an object it is going to manifest a difference within the object, either by breaking the object in pieces or by establishing a new birth within the object that was never seen before. Every season is good and made for a benefit for the land but an extension of one season to continue throughout the duration of the other season's time to manifest can never be good for the earth. The Targets for this Sixth Book is Everyone, Man and Woman, Rich and Poor, Kings and Queens, Presidents and Prime Ministers, Judges and Lawyers, Wise and Fools, Educated and Dunce, Principals and Vice Principals, Altars and Non-Altars, Christians and Non-Christians, Bishops and Pastors, Brothers and Sisters, Child and Babes, High and Lows. There must be a time to take a clear look at life, if not for ourselves, then definitely for the life that we care about. No man is fixed to do what another man is doing, each man has his own journey to establish his own purpose for life. For those who will find the interest of reading this Book Called "GOD'S UGLY", I pray that you would have found some valuable life changing instructions that will help to fashion your future and also to bring forth a Divine Coverage within your preparation for every Storms of GOD'S UGLY. God Bless.

INTRODUCTION

Greetings to All in The Wonderful Name of Jesus Christ, Lord and King, from Spiritual to Physical then back to The Spiritual. The Servant of God in the person of Pastor Lerone Dinnall and The Ministry of The Church of Jesus Christ Fellowship in Jamaica presents to the world another Breathtaking, Life Changing, Instructions Filled and evidence of God's Divine Anointing within a Book, that will be sure to act as A Spiritual Compass for the souls of man, for the development of people, for the Spiritual Strength of a city and country and for the True path of a man's destiny for the beyond. This Book with the title being: " **GOD'S UGLY** " is book number six from Pastor Lerone Dinnall and The Ministry of The Church of Jesus Christ Fellowship in Jamaica.

GOD'S UGLY was burnt from The Spirit of God within my vessel to manifest a sense of Spiritual Guidelines that may have been known to many or may have not been known by some, but it is certain that all will know what are the spirits destructive paths within mankind that will establish The Rage of God's Divine Spirit to Move with Vengeance to Execute His Anger upon people, places and things of the earth.

This Book is Unique from all the other books that I have written for The Ministry of God, because within this book it will be identified that The Lord Instructed for this book to be established in three different Phases to manifest within the physical of a man of what exactly is the three different steps within The Spiritual of God's Divine Authority. Phase One of this book with The Title being: GOD'S UGLY is called: The Beginning, The Manifestation and

3

Nature of The Father… and it represents The Highest Level within The Divine Authority of God's Order. Phase One has eight Messages that are put together to express The All Spirituality of The Father, that which The Father is in Agreement with, that which The Father is not in Agreement with, It establishes the once position of lucifer and the final position of lucifer, it expresses the first sin of The Spiritual before there was any other sins that was birth. Phase One clearly identifies the true face of the rules of this world and pinpoints the weakness of its strength because of the dependability for the feeding of spirits instead of The True Worship to The Sovereign King. It identifies exactly what must be done and maintained for any Child of God to be and to remain being Accepted for God's Divine Flow and also encourages A Child of God to know their true position in this life and in The Spiritual Life to remain **FIX** in that Position that God Has Manifested for that Child of God to manifest their purpose continually in.

Phase Two of this Beautiful Book is Called: The Body, The Son of God, Jesus Christ, The Direct Divine Link and Only Access from The Divine Spiritual to The Physical, The Divine Mediator, The Second Adam, The Second Manifestation from The Highest Authority of God… Phase Two has Seven Sword and Soul piercing Messages that will reflect The Spirituality of God's View. Within this phase of the book it will be identified WHAT Is The Authority, WHO Is The Authority, The Three Steps Within The Authority, How can The Authority be Identified, and how should The Authority be Used by A Child of God. Through reading and Spiritually understanding this book it will be discovered by A Child of God what are and who are those who have been using and continue to use an authority that is not complete, or is of the wrong manifestation from that of God Being The Divine Head. This Phase is called The Body for a reason because its job is to establish all that will be manifested within the vessel of A Child of God through Spiritual Divine Connection from The Father, and also to identify to A Child of God exactly that which must never be invited within our vessel for manifestation, and power is truly ours to choose that which we have given access for the birth of its cemented manifestations.

Phase Two of this Inspiring Book ends with highlighting to mankind of that which is our greatest challenge in this life, some may think that it's the conceiving from The Spiritual the unseen iniquity or the actual actions of a sin, but The Divine Godhead Reveals that God Already Knew that we would sin, therefore, sin is not the greatest offense but rather our buried discipline of finding The Spiritual Hunger of needing to make certain that we have confessed the sins that have been committed by ourselves from The Spiritual to The physical manifestation of our vessel.

Phase Three of this Spiritual Education for life is called: THE CLOSING, The Divine Prophecies from The Speech of The Holy Ghost... Phase Three has Five Solid Messages of Warning for God's People and for those who govern to establish rule for the earth.

This Phase of the book expresses The First Divine Step within The Authority of God through the Speech of The Holy Ghost for Divine Spiritual Access to be Granted from our Father that Sits In The Supremacy of All Divine Authority that is **FIXED**. Reading through this phase of the book, it will be identified again that choice is freely given for a man to accept that which is prophesied or to reject that which is written to warn against that which is to come for any man, people, nation, country and even for The Church that finds themselves on The Wrong Side of God. It's not by my will to write these prophecies within a Book that I've Received through Visions and God Speaking through me, but rather it is The Spirit of God that Burns with Divine Approval to give a witness to the world a Living Testimony from a Vessel that is still alive, to acknowledge to all, that this is The Word that The Lord Has Spoken as A Warning to All to demonstrate exactly what The Sovereign God Will Do if Spiritual Guidelines are abused, if Spiritual Rules are broken, If Unrighteousness is placed where Righteousness should be fixed,

If Covenants are broken and if God's Divine Will for this life is not carefully observed. It Is A Warning To All!

I encourage all who will read this Spiritual Book to Pray first and ask your Father which has All Power to Reveal within your own vessels if this Manuscript is fulfilling The Will and Direction of The God of The Entire Universe. And if there is truly a Relationship with your Father, then it is certain as The Sun Shineth to Acknowledge Covenant for The Righteous, that your Father Will Never Give an Answer that will Manifest that His Children Will be Led In The Direction of Confusions that will end in the sure Destruction of His Child.

St Matthew Chapter 7:7-11.

"Ask, and it shall be given you; seek, and ye shall find; knock, and it shall be opened unto you: For every one that asketh receiveth; and he that seeketh findeth; and to him that knocketh it shall be opened. Or what man is there of you, whom if his son ask bread, will he give him a stone? Or if he ask a fish, will he give him a Serpent? If ye then, being evil, know how to give good gifts unto your children, how much more shall your Father which is in Heaven Give Good Things to them that ask Him"?

With The Word of God, The Introduction of this Blessed Book being GOD'S UGLY is concluded. My continual prayer for all God's People is to be Spiritually Covered and Abide within The Guidelines of God's Covenant then it will always be seen that God's Ugly can never Affect God's Beauty. From The Ministry of The Church of Jesus Christ Fellowship, Savannah Cross, Jamaica, West Indies. From Your Brother, A Friend, God's Servant, Pastor Lerone Dinnall. Amen.

OPENING SCRIPTURES

Exodus Chapter 14:21-28.

And Moses stretched out his hand over the sea; and The Lord caused the sea to go back by a strong east wind all that night, and made the sea dry land, and the waters were divided. And the children of Israel went into the midst of the sea upon the dry ground: and the waters were a wall unto them on their right hand, and on their left. And the Egyptians pursued, and went in after them to the midst of the sea, even all Pharaoh's horses, his chariots, and his horsemen. And it came to pass, that in the morning watch The Lord Looked unto the host of the Egyptians through the pillar of fire and of the clouds, and troubled the host of the Egyptians, And Took off their chariot wheels, that they drave them heavily: so that the Egyptians said, let us flee from the face of Israel; for The Lord Fighteth for them against the Egyptians. And The Lord Said unto Moses, Stretch out thine hand over the sea, that the waters may come again upon the Egyptians, upon their chariots, and upon their horsemen. And Moses stretched forth his hand over the sea, and the sea returned to his strength when the morning appeared; and the Egyptians fled against it; and The Lord Overthrew the Egyptians in the midst of the sea. And the waters returned, and covered the chariots, and the horsemen, and all the host of Pharaoh that came into the sea after them; there remained not so much as one of them.

Numbers Chapter 16:28-35.

And Moses said, Hereby ye shall know that The Lord hath sent me to do all these works; for I have not done them of mine own mind. If these men die the common death of all men, or if they be visited after the visitation of all men; then The Lord hath not sent me. But if The Lord make a New Thing, and the earth open her mouth, and swallow them up, with all that appertain unto them, and they go down quick into the pit; then ye shall understand that these men have provoked The Lord. And it came to pass, as he had made an end of speaking all these words, that the ground clave asunder that was under them: And the earth opened her mouth, and swallowed them up, and their houses, and all the men that appertained unto Korah, and all their goods. They, and all that appertained to them, went down alive into the pit, and the earth closed upon them: and they perished from among the congregation. And all Israel that were round about them fled at the cry of them: for they said, Lest the earth swallow us up also. And there came out fire from The Lord, and Consumed the two hundred and fifty men that offered incense.

MINDSET

- It's always a good thing to know where the limits of an object is; It's even better to know what are the pressure points of The God that we serve or don't serve!

- Truth is not something that is expressed by a person's mouth but rather, Truth is identified in that which out lives life and death!

- The manifestation of Truth is dependent on that which a person is trained to become, therefore, if training cannot stand up to The Spiritual Quality of God's Truth, then Training is made waste based on that which was a person's belief of their original truth!

- Truth is not real because of support from many people, but Truth is identified to be True because it passes the Test of Spiritual to Physical then back to Spiritual!

- It's never wise for mankind to create an atmosphere where it is seen that God The Creator of all things is in a Position of being Angry, there are always some great life changing consequences to follow that will take effect in the continuation of whatever a man desires as life that is being lived!

- To Understand eventually births Knowledge, and to have Knowledge Complete is to birth the Wisdom to know what to do with that Knowledge!

- To be in a Position to advance a thing or to stop a thing is called being responsibly, but to be in the Position and have the Knowledge of what is Facts from that which is Friction and do nothing to advance and build to grow that which is Facts, that is called being careless!

- Starting all over from zero is never an easy task if it's even possible in life's current state, but having some solid materials to build a foundation even stronger is better than continuing to build anything that truly has no foundation!

- When The Lord Moves with Anger it's never a movement of half accomplishing that which is set out to be fulfilled, but rather, it is a Movement of completing that which is destined for God's Destruction!

- If a vessel is full it has to run over, if God's Anger Has Peaked it must be Manifested!

- It's Always a good time for Repentance, fools ignore the speech and thoughts of repentance but the wise will always embrace the action of Repentance because they are aware of the Facts!

- Everything is subjected to change because of the governance of spirits to feed, Truth from God is the only real virtue that will never change because God's Governance is Spiritually Sustainable without Physical beginning and ending, therefore, God's Truth doesn't require feeding to remove or to change that which is already God's Spiritual Truth!

- Having an umbrella in the rain is of great convenience to prevent from becoming wet, so is it for a man's soul to be identified under The Spiritual Coverage of God's Divine

Protection whenever A Spiritual Storm is sent forth to destroy!

- It's always important to know The Spiritual Value of remaining in the ship!

- The Divine Steps within The Authority of God are 100% Spiritually what it is, being Divinely Strong and Unbreakable and always requires Divine Access from The Father to move from One Access of God's Authority to another Access of God's Authority and then to The Final Access of God's Divine Authority!

- Ugly is not a good word, but whenever it is manifested by The Father it always Births God's Will Being Done!

- Try not to experience God's Ugly, a person distant from Spiritual Coverage may not live to tell the story!

- It's Always a good time to pray, when trouble comes it will be Spiritually Satisfying to know that prayer was already being stored up and continuing to be made to The Father, rather than just beginning the start of prayer because of what is now happening and is about to happen!

- That which Moves God to Anger is always a direction from people, places and things to establish upon the land that which is in contradiction of God's Divine Will Being Done, moving out of design and true purpose. Truth!

- It's Always an excellent thing to know the Name of your Savior, rather than just repeating the title God, He Has A Saving Name. Do you know it? _____.
The Saving Name for our God Is Jesus Christ!

Artwork from Ministry: Turn On The Light

Art Work Done
by Pastor Leonie
Lumsall.

March 10, 2022.

LET US TURN ON
The LigHT FOR
GOD'S UGLY.

PHASE ONE

**The Beginning; The Manifestation and
The Nature of The Father...
The Third and Final Step or Access
within The Authority of God.**

THE NATURE OF GOD...

Message # 69
Date Started March 17, 2017
Date Finalized March 17, 2017.

Revelation Chapter 1:8.

"I Am Alpha and Omega, The Beginning and
The Ending, saith The Lord, which Is, and which
Was, and which is To Come, The Almighty".

Revelation Chapter 1:17&18.

"And when I saw Him, I fell at His Feet as dead. And
he laid His Right Hand upon me, saying unto me, Fear
not; I Am The First and The Last: I Am He that Liveth,
and was dead; and behold, I Am Alive for evermore,
Amen; and have the keys of hell and of death".

Exodus Chapter 3:14.

"And God said unto Moses, I AM THAT I AM:
and he said, thus shalt thou say unto the children
of Israel, I AM hath sent me unto you".

1 Kings Chapter 20:23-28.

"And the servants of the king of Syria said unto him, their gods are gods of the hills; therefore they were stronger than we; but let us fight against them in the plain, and surely we shall be stronger than they. And do this thing, take the Kings away, every man out of his place, and put captains in their rooms: and number thee an army, like the army that thou hast lost, horse for horse, and chariot for chariot: and we will fight against them in the plain, and surely we shall be stronger than they. And he hearkened unto their voice, and did so. And it came to pass at the return of the year, that Benhadad numbered the Syrians, and went up to Aphek, to fight against Israel. And the children of Israel were numbered, and were all present, and went against them: and the children of Israel pitched before them like two little flocks of kids; but the Syrians filled the country. And there came a man of God, and spake unto the king of Israel, and said, thus saith The Lord, because the Syrians have said, The Lord is God of the hills, but he is not God of the valleys, therefore will I deliver all this great multitude into thine hand, and ye shall know that I Am The Lord".

2 Chronicles Chapter 20:14-17.

"Then upon Jahaziel the son of Zechariah, the son of Benaiah, the son of Jeiel, the son of Mattaniah, a Levite of the sons of Asaph, came The Spirit of The Lord in the Midst of the congregation; and he said, hearken ye, all Judah, and ye inhabitants of Jerusalem, and thou king Jehoshaphat, thus saith The Lord unto you, be not afraid nor be dismayed by reason of this great multitude; for the battle is not yours, but God's. Tomorrow go ye down against them: behold, they come up by the cliff of Ziz; and ye shall find them at the end of the brook, before the wilderness of Jeruel. Ye shall not have need to fight in this battle: set yourselves,

stand still, and see the salvation of the Lord with you, O Judah and Jerusalem: fear not, nor be dismayed; tomorrow go out against them: for The Lord will be with you".

I Greet all my Father's Children in The Wonderful Matchless Name of Jesus Christ our Soon Coming King. Privileged and Honored am I to be in this Position to write and to Inspire the Children of The Living God. Here we have a Topic, which is more than A Message, it can be identified to that of A Revelation I got in A Vision, when I was in my bed.

I had A Vision on the 10 th of March 2017, and in that Vision, I went to A Church with the members of my Assembly, This Church was not like any other Church I have been to, because I could not describe the Nature of The Church, seeing that it was without length and breath, and it was that all God's People could have perfectly fit into that Church; every Bishops with their Righteous Assembly, every Pastors, every Overseer, every Ministers and Missionaries along with all The Righteous Generation of God. If you were to ask me how could that many people fit in one Assembly, I would not have an answer to give; but this I can say: all things are Possible with God. I'm not even certain if I saw any walls or structure of a Building, because there were so many people; and also The Church had no roof or ceiling, and there was no danger of rain interrupting the Service, because God The Commander and Chief is The Head of all Actions that should take place.

Upon entering The Church Assembly, and having taken our seat on the Right of The Church Assembly, a Servant of God who was occupying the Position to be the Master of the Service then stopped the Service to Acknowledge that Pastor Lerone Dinnall and the Saints from The Church of Jesus Christ Fellowship Savannah Cross is present in the Assembly; after doing this I witness the silence of all the Saints, which is ironic, because when we are introduced to an Assembly, it is the custom that all the other Assembly would then make an applause to welcome an Assembly of God. This did not take place; what happened was complete silence, then there appeared the Manifestation of an Upper Level, and that Person that was Sitting at the Upper Level Looked down to witness for Himself, that, that which was announced was correct; this Person in the Nature of being a Man, got up, and began to move in the direction of the Assembly of The Righteous; in what way this man came from the Upper room to now being in the Assembly of The Righteous, that I cannot tell, and it remains a Mystery; but this I can say, it was like He Floated from The Upper Room down to the Assembly of The Righteous.

Now what I'm going to Reveal is the Foundation of The Topic that is given, which is called: The Nature of God. The Appearance of this Man was unlike anything else anyone have ever seen to reveal, neither have I seen this Manifestation or Revelation of this type in The Bible; but the more I reflect on that which I have seen, I came to the realization that this is a Manifestation and A Unique Nature of God. When this Man Floated from the Upper Room to the Assembly of The Righteous, I looked to see if I could Identify Who it was that was coming from The Upper Room, and now moving in a Direction to come towards where I am; when I looked, I discovered that the Man was very short, but something took place as He took one step at a time; the Man began to Grow in Stature; and not only did He began to Grow in Stature, but when I Looked to see if I could Identify Who this Man was, I discovered that at one appearance, as this Man made one step, He grew in Stature and also His Facial recognition Change; meaning, at one appearance when I looked, He was a Black Man and very Short; with another step He took, He became a Chinese Man, and became a little taller; with one more step, this Man Manifested and became a White Man and got taller; and with each step, this man became taller and also changed the Manifestation of the Nature that He was at first; at the time this Man came before me to the right hand of The Church Assembly, He was now three (3) or Four (4) times the high of my Stature, in that I had to be looking up, as if I was looking up into the Sun.

The Man was very tall, and when I looked to identify now what was the Manifestation or the Nature of The Man, when I Looked I discovered that His Face was not easily Identify, because it was like a screening that covered the clarity of what His Features truly are, but I could identify that His Face was not of one skin complexion nor His Nature of one Nationality, but it was instead a mixture of all complexions and a mixture of all Nationalities all in One Man. Therefore I could not look and say of a surety, that this Man is a Black man, or a White man, or Chinese, or Japanese, or African; This Man was In All Nationalities and in all People and in all Customs, in all levels of Stature; and it was perfectly Clear that He Had all Power to Manifest into whatever Culture to Reach and to Save all the Nations of the World. The only thing I did not discover in this Vision is the speaking of Different Language from this Man.

At the time when this Man came before me being very tall; He opened His Mouth and said:

"Welcome, You Have Made It"!

I can't tell my Readers if this was a Vision of the upcoming Rapture, but the Nature of the events felt like something very special. At the time when this Man Said Welcome, you have made it; I then discovered that He Formed His Right Fist, and right over my head He Punch what was discovered afterwards to be a glass; upon placing one punch through that glass, I heard a loud smash, that made my heart raced even in the Vision, I then discovered the splinters of glass falling from over my head unto the ground, in hundreds of pieces; Then the very Tall Man Said to me:

**"YOUR TEST IS COMPLETED, ALL
YOUR ENEMIES ARE SHATTERED
LIKE THE GLASS ON THE GROUND,
YOU HAVE OVERCOME"!**

Saints I didn't even know that there was a glass over my head that represented a Test, that wherever I went, it followed me, up until The Lord Saw it fit to Remove the Test of which I face. It was then in the Vision I discovered that this Man wasn't any ordinary Man, this Man that Changed Nationalities and Grew from small to tall, was not a Man or a Bishop, or Pastor or Angel; this Man that was found Worthy to be in The Upper Room was in Fact **THE GOD OF THE UNIVERSE.**

Then God Looked on me and Smiled, and Turned, and went back to where He was coming from, and as He was Going, I discovered that He became smaller with every step away He Made and also Changing Nationalities; then I Discovered that this was Indeed a Revelation of the Manifestation of The King of kings and The Lord of lords, Jesus Christ The Saviour of the whole World. Then I awoke out of my Vision.

From that very day I awoke from that Vision, it was like A Fresh Anointing, the removal of an unbearable load that has been lifted; every problem that came my way from that time to present, was like butter to the very hot Sun, it just melted away. Problem! What Problem? Each time Problem comes from now onwards, I will show my problems to The God that have Shattered my enemies like the smashing of a Glass in hundreds of pieces.

I Truly hope that this Message would have benefited those who would have read. As always, Now and Forevermore, all my Praise, Glory and Honour, is for The King of kings and The Lord of lords, Jesus Christ The Saviour of Mankind. From The Ministry of The Church of Jesus Christ Fellowship, Savannah Cross, Jamaica, West Indies. Pastor Lerone Dinnall. God's Blessings Continually.

The Nature Of God...

UNINVITE SPIRITS!

Message # 157   Date Started September 16, 2020
                                    Date Finalized September 16, 2020.

Let's Begin With Prayer...

"Father of Heaven and Earth I come before Your Presence this night in The Name of Jesus Christ asking for Your Continual Forgiveness for the sins of the past, the sins of the present and also for all the sins of the future, even those sins that my children would have committed and also those sins that their children would have committed, this I humbly ask in The Name of Jesus Christ. Father, I pray that You will always Allow Your People to be aware of the importance of Your Divine Approval for our lives which can only be Released because You Have Seen it fit through the manifestations of our actions to Release those Favors. Father, Help us to seek You with all our Hearts, Might and Soul to do that which pleases Your Will for our lives.

Father, I have accepted the fact that there is no direction unless You have Spoken The Speech for direction to be made. Father, You are Sovereign over my life, therefore I humbly wait on Your Guidance to point in the path of Righteousness of Your Kingdom Being Established within my life.

Father, as we seek to explore a topic of this nature, I Pray that Your Divine Intelligence Will Speak through my fingers that those who have read will completely understand and

acknowledge that these words are manifesting from Your Spirit. Father, You Alone Is God and none can be compared to You; It wasn't seen in Eternity, it was never manifested in the past, the present day bares no record of it, therefore the future already dictates to those of us who are observing now to know that it can never be established, and when this life has had its full course because time will be all used up, Sovereignty will still be Yours in the Realms of Eternity. In The Name of Jesus Christ to God Be All Glory, Honor and Praise, Forever to Eternity, Amen".

Greetings again to all God's Beautiful People, God's Grace and Mercy has brought me through, I'm happy to find myself again in this position of Heaven's Worth to Inspire the lives of God's People. It's amazing to see the effects of words, especially The Word that is Spoken from The Mouth of God. The Bible Declares and Decrees that The Lord Uses His Words to form the Heavens and the Earth, He Used Words and everything was immediately fitted to its correct position of purpose for His Will Being Done. Therefore we get to understand that The Word of God Carries The Divine Order of God to wherever that Word is sent to.

I always tell people that question me about these messages to find themselves in some type of meaningful relationship with God by doing for themselves some Fastings and Prayers and then observing for themselves if what God Said was somehow different from what I have written in that which God Asked me to write. The Facts remain that every person can seek The Face of God for themselves, actually, God Is Moved with joy through the actions of His Children to hear exactly what God Said to them. We need to understand very quickly before time has ran out that this world is daily teaching and training our minds to believe that there is no God, and if those of us who knows for a surety that there is A God decides to keep our mouths shut, then it's only a limited time before this world's poison has caught up to us to choke the seed of belief that we have inside of us to demonstrate that there is truly A Sovereign God.

We are currently living in a world that is filled with the manifestations of spirits, spirits are only dangerous if there is not given The Approval By Spirit to know how to contain the movements and effects of spirits. This means that if spirits are left unchecked and continue to feed, then spirits will develop and become demons and legions of that very environment of which it now exists in. There are many Saints of God that are unaware of spirits in their current environment because spirits will always seek to hide if it is threatened by the environment's light, this meaning that many times something that did happen never really happened when it is found that the presence of A Child of God is around that environment. It's important to also identify to God's People that spirits must be invited within the environment of which it is found to be occupying, whether by willful invitation or through the means of invitation under a disguise, it still spells within The Spiritual that an Invitation was granted for spirits to move in to thus occupy the space in which it must now penetrate.

The Lord Revealed to me that spirits are always hungry for possession, meaning that once spirits have found themselves to occupy a space within the environment close to potential lights for God's Glory, those spirits will fight to keep that space to thus try to advance it's movements of feeding. The Lord Revealed to me that spirits love a clean temple because within a clean temple is also found Authority from God which means Approval from God. Yes, The Gifts from The Father can be overwhelmed by the spirit's acceptance within that temple through the means of the same power of invitation of those spirits by the occupant of that temple. To understand spirits being A Child of God is to understand manifestation, if A Child of God doesn't understand manifestation then it has become even more difficult for that Child of God to know exactly what's the next move of spirits within their environment. The Lord Revealed to me that spirits have three main points within the life of A Child of God that they must seek to try and penetrate and will always seek at all times to focus on these three main gates of A Child of God.

1. spirits must seek to inject its influence in The Spiritual of A Child of God which means A Child of God's Altar manifested to God, if spirits can cause some changes to how A Child of God Worships their Father then the penetration would have began, a little leaven leaveneth the whole lump.

2. spirits must seek to inject its influence within the family of A Child of God, if the family is affected it means that the continuation of that Child of God is being restricted based on spirits seed that has been sown within that family.

3. spirits must seek to inject its influence within the finance of A Child of God which means your money, and this is the most challenging of all because money's spirit is govern by movement therefore it has to move, where it now move to and comes from, A Child of God has to be extremely careful and Spiritually Focused of when money is moving because money is always moving with spirits and there is really nothing we can do about that, but it will be found at times that some money has an increased influence of spirits movement which comes with the manifestation of seeking to destroy those who have received of that fixed money. As I said before that spirit's only Governor is Spirit meaning The Spirit of God, therefore A Child of God that is Spiritually Linked with their Father will know exactly at what time it is that their finance has been affected with forces of over-whelming spirit's destruction of their finance. Here is a secret that The Lord Revealed to me: Never find your-self putting money together, especially those money of which you're not certain of its origin, this means that you will always have your personal means of earnings but when it is seen that other earnings have entered your surroundings by means of work done by you, it's

never wise to now put those fresh earnings with foundation source of earnings because if spirits is attacking you're finance of which it will, when those earnings are placed with the foundation earnings it will become like spiritual caterpillars eating away the true strength of your earnings by the same access of invitation, and this is why this type of attack by spirits is so dangerous because everyone has to seek to earn to make a living for themselves and their family. The Lord Revealed to me that if A Child of God's Altar is Strong in God then that strength of that Altar would have automatically canceled the effect of how dangerous spirits can truly manifest for the destruction of A Child of God. You've Been Warned!

Uninvite spirits, How does A Child of God uninvite something that at times we don't even know that it is there?_____
_____. This is what The Lord Revealed to me: spirits is also known in The Bible as **UNCLEAN**, which means that even though it has a type of pattern which seek to replicate itself as The Spirit of God's First Manifestation which is to **MOVE**, unclean spirits cannot move to function in an environment that A Child of God has made to be Spiritually Clean, and if Spiritually Clean it means that it is Spiritually Strong. And that's what A Child of God has to learn effectively from God. How do I find myself to become Spiritually Clean and remain to be Spiritually Clean? If it is that this same Child of God needs to uninvite spirits from their surroundings which is our Altar for God, our Family's continuation and also our Finance. If we can get Clean and get our Altar Clean, get our Family Clean then it will automatically bring forth Divine Coverage for our Finance to cancel the destruction of spirits flow of feeding. How do I get Clean?_____
_____. The only way and path for A Christian to become Spiritually Clean must point in the direction of purposeful **FASTING**, without Fasting there can be no Spiritual Cleansing, it's like putting your Soul in God's Washing

Machine with the soap being that of God's Blood, the Only Blood that was shed to remove sin completely. This advice is for the person that sees themselves to understand that Spiritual Deliverance can only be activated by that same person, meaning that no one can be cleansed for another person, you would have to do the True Clean Sacrifice of Fasting to Seek God's Face yourself. It's good when others pray for us, it's even great when we can do it for ourselves.

I Hope God's People have been Spiritually Inspired by this message, again I Declare and Decree that All Glory be Offered to The Only God that Sits High and Looks Low, to The God of All Secrets, In The Name of Jesus Christ Receive All my Praise, Amen. From Pastor Lerone Dinnall and The Ministry of The Church of Jesus Christ Fellowship Savannah Cross, May Pen, Clarendon, Jamaica, West Indies. God Bless.

"spirits, You're Not Welcome In My Surroundings In The Name of Jesus Christ, Amen"!

SPIRITUAL GOVERNANCE OR IS IT

"SPIRITUAL GOVERNANCE", CHOOSE...

Message # 152

Date Started August 30, 2020.
Date Finalized September 1, 2020.

St John Chapter 15:7.

"If ye abide in Me, and My Words abide in you, ye shall ask what ye will, and it shall be done unto you".

Blessing to all God's Beautiful People, again this is a great opportunity for myself to be in this Position to write words of Spiritual Growth that will Inspire the lives of God's People. God Is Good, God Is Great, God Is Merciful, God Is Forgiving, God Is Love, God Is A Friend, God Is Always Ready to Listen and Always Happy to Help, to God Be All The Glory Great and Mighty Things He Has Done, Amen.

I learned this Topic from The Intelligence of God, there are sometimes on this journey God Will Immediately Tell A Child of God to Look! Meaning to see something that you would not necessarily see if The Lord Had Not Pointed it out to your Spirit. Within The Teaching of The Almighty God there are always Spiritual Benefits to receive and A Child of God is always receiving more than that which that Child of God was expecting to receive from The Hands of God.

Everything in this life in which we live is functioned under The Authority of Spiritual Governance or a spiritual governance, it's either we are knowledgeable of this fact or we are not knowledgeable. To receive the Understanding of a thing is to receive The Spiritual Key of that same thing in which you have now gained the understanding of, without the perfect understanding of anything it means that we have no Spiritual Key to unlock the continual mystery of The Unknown Revelations. Governance is speaking about rules and a fixed control in which something is to operate within the guidance of that same rule, and spiritual is always referring to those things that the natural eyes can never see.

It is clear as day to identify that not a lot of people or Saints of God understand what the terms Spiritual Governance or spiritual governance actually means. I hope when we have gone through this Topic we will receive a greater understanding of what we face daily and are not fully aware of what is really taking place. The home that a person lives in carries either a Spiritual Governance or a spiritual governance, the husband and the wife that we choose to marry will manifest the same Spiritual Governance or a spiritual governance, the place where we work has the sure manifestation of Spiritual Governance or spiritual governance and most important, the altar that we present our sacrifice on has a governance, whether it is The Spiritual Governance of The Father or it's going to be the spiritual governance of spirits, demons, lodge, necromancy, powers of the dark altars.

The Spiritual Governance of The Father has the Manifestation at all times to establish Spiritual Growth for every Child of God. This means that once A Child of God is within The Spiritual Governance of their Father there will be No Limits to that which that Child of God can obtain from their Father, because God Has No Limits, there is No Measurements to be found from The Manifestation of The Authority of God. On the other side or Spiritually Viewing, below the Manifestation of Spiritual Governance is the spiritual governance, now each person has to understand that every spirit is granted permission to operate at the level to which it must operate and cannot go further beyond that which it is entitled to operate at, thus it is seen and must manifest that those who have found themselves under the guidance of spiritual governance, these are the same persons that has to manifest within the rules and laws of that which that spirit of governance is granted permission to operate at and nothing more.

Now because of the fixed limitations of spiritual governance a person under the influence of this governance can never find themselves excelling above that fixed barrier. I was working at a place and I never knew then what I know now. In the past working for this company I realized that whenever someone desired to go further than that position in which that person have found themselves to perform for this company, I realized that the message from all those who were of the system of the spiritual governance was to discourage such a person by painting a picture within the life of this person which would suggest that there is absolutely no opportunity for anyone who desires to move outside the walls of that which they have come to now pattern within the walls of the same spiritual governance. Has I said before, what I Know now, if I Knew it then, I would have fast tracked all my plans at earlier dates but I've Learnt from The Father that A Child of God should never regret the past because it stands as a main tool for Education for that same Child of God's Experience and Journey in life. The Lord Said:

The Lord Speaks...

**"We Should Rather Look Back Within Our Minds
To Repent And Not To Regret, Thus Bringing Fourth
Change For Present Life And The Future Life,
Because The Example Of The Past Life Is One
Of The Main Tools For Training"!**

It is no secret that spirit's governance lives off the fear of those who they are governing, the moment a person that was found under the management of spiritual governance realizes that there is in fact an higher level to be found in God, it is at that moment that such a person would have broken the limitations from off their minds to now step into The Unknown of God's Endless Opportunity which has No Walls, No Barriers, No Limits and No Restrictions.

If a person or Child of God remains under spiritual governance's rule, then it is expected that such a person or Child of God have already cemented their growth to that which their spiritual governance now dictates. A Child of God has to understand that if you're not Growing Spiritually in whatever you're being governed by, then you have no one to blame but yourself. What I'm encouraging The people of God to know is that God Never Plants A Child of God to Remain at the same Position in life, there is always Movements and Growth for the life of God's Children. And if A Child of God is not finding that Spiritual Movement which leads to Sure Spiritual Growth then that Child of God should start evaluating themselves and also their **WORTH IN GOD**.

It is important to identify to God's People that if the spiritual governance of our lives have never received the approval from God to advance to level 2, then those who are under the guidance of their approval will never receive the support to move from their governance to achieve a higher level of Spiritual Approval. Every Child of God has a Sure Destiny in God, this destiny however can never be achieved while that Child of God remains under the influence of spiritual governance.

There are many spiritual governance that are known and there are many spiritual governance that are not known to A Child of God, therefore we are defeated because we don't know what are the spirits that are governing everything that we come in contact with. I've learned this only through experience of life and God Asking me to **LOOK!**

What Am I Looking For I Asked?_____.

- **LOOK and UNDERSTAND! Don't you see that the Internet is functioned and mastered by a spiritual governance!**

- **LOOK and UNDERSTAND! Don't you see that the Television programs and Radio programs are under the control of a spiritual governance!**

- **LOOK and UNDERSTAND! Don't you see that even those who are in the position to represent people in government, don't you see that they are operating under the influence of spiritual governance!**

- **LOOK and UNDERSTAND! The Banks are fixed with the true face of spiritual governance!**

- **LOOK and UNDERSTAND! All systems implemented by man outside of The Leading of Almighty God are already under the governance of spiritual authorities!**

- **LOOK and UNDERSTAND! That person that you call your friend, if they remain under the influence of spiritual governance, can they really be a friend to assist your life to Spiritually Grow?**

A Child of God has to choose for themselves their own pathway that leads to Spiritual Growth or no growth. When I really think about it, it comes back to The Sure Relationship that A Child of God will maintain for themselves and God. If There is An Active Relationship with God it means that there is always A Spiritual Burning that **MUST** Crave Spiritual Growth, thus this same Child of God will never find themselves remaining under the influences of spiritual governance because there can be **NO SPIRITUAL GROWTH** under the influence of spiritual governance.

To The Father Above Be All Glory, Honor and Praise from Everlasting to Eternity in The Name of Jesus Christ, Amen. I hope The People of God received something that is Spiritually Important for the lives of God's Chosen. From Pastor Lerone Dinnall and The Ministry of The Church of Jesus Christ Fellowship, Savannah Cross, May Pen, Clarendon, Jamaica, West Indies. God's Blessing Always In The Name of Jesus Christ.

Embrace Spiritual Governance!
Put On Your Spiritual Shoes
And Run Away From

"spiritual governance"!

You've Been Warned!

I KNOW THE FACE OF THE DEVIL...

Message # 81

Date Started December 2, 2018
Date Finalized December 2, 2018.

I Give Honor and Glory to The Most Excellent Father; In no other Name than The Name that is Highly Exalted above all other names, through The Mighty Name of Jesus Christ I Give Praise. I am Blessed to be in this Position that I can be an available Instrument for God's Glory.

Our Experience in Life is one that we must never shy away from; because it is that same experience that is going to enable us to have The Spiritual Strength that we require to be able to Manifest The Authority of The Living God in everything that we must seek to Overcome in this life.

There are times it will be Observed that our experiences cause us to be Broken, Battered, Bruised, Burnt and also Drowned; because of that which we are scheduled to be a part of, to thus fulfill our Purpose in God. But everything in life carries a scar whether Spiritual or Physical; it leaves an Impression on the lives of those who must endure their Process to find the surety of their future through Divine Purpose.

After we have Endured and Overcome our Experience, it leaves us with A Testimony, that we can share with others, to enable us to

Teach, Preach, and Encourage those who must now travel on their Journey, to be Prepared for what is Ahead; thus Preparing the Future Generations for all the Trials that they must now be well Educated to Overcome.

For My Personal Experience, I've discovered that at all times when I'm misguided, and have gone on a pathway that leads to complete and utmost Failure, I discovered that the Conditions of that Failure has a Pattern, and this pattern will not be learnt in one Failure, but rather, it often takes a lot of Failures for us to understand the Pattern of why we do Fail. If we are Chosen by God to Stop from Failing, and Start to Overcome to Succeed, then The Lord Will Enable for A Child of God to begin Discerning the conditions of their own life, to thus discover why it is that they would always be finding themselves in Traps and Bondages.

The Lord Revealed to me that at all times when I Failed; I must discover that it was the same Environment that keeps repeating itself, and that Environment was based on the Facts that I did not as yet Overcome the level of that Environment to then cause me to succeed. That Environment that caused me to continually Failed was a Condition of Rush, that sees those who are offering the Opportunity, they are desiring for A Child of God to Sign the deal of that Opportunity without looking into that which they are signing a deal for; thus Manifesting A Big Trap and Snare for the devil to place on those who have not taken the time to Analyze the Opportunity that is placed before them.

I know the face of the devil. The Lord Revealed that A Child of God will only be aware of what the devil is doing, only through Complete Trust of their own life with The Father Above. Trust for God Will Establish Relationship with God, therefore ensuring that A Child of God's Movement is Directed by The Wave of The Spirit of God.

The Lord Revealed that as long as A Child of God is within Purpose for God, then The Lord through Relationship with that Child of God

Will Release A Fresh Anointing, that will see that Servant now being Able to Overcome their Past Failures of the Same Opportunities that they were in fact always at a disadvantage, because of a Lack of Relationship with The Father Above. The Lord Revealed that without Relationship, there will be no Anointing Released for A Child of God to Overcome the Traps and Snares of Opportunities that presents itself.

What is the face of the devil?

Answer: OPPORTUNITIES WITHOUT GOD'S DIRECTION, TRUTH!

These are opportunities that are placed in front of A Child of God that Lacks Relationship with Their Father. Relationship with God will always Manifest to A Child of God, that, in whatever Opportunities that is Offered, there will always be A Constant Presence with That Child of God to know that The Alpha and Omega is always Present in every avenue of that Child of God's Decisions. Thus Manifesting Perfect Intelligence Available to A Child of God, to thus Overcome the Negative effects of every Opportunities that is on the pathway of A Child of God.

We are Encourage with The Words of God Which States:

Proverbs Chapter 3:5-10.

"Trust in The Lord with all thine heart; and lean not unto thine own understanding. In all thy ways acknowledge Him, and He Will Direct thy paths. Be not wise in thine own eyes: fear The Lord, and depart from evil. It shall be health to thy navel, and marrow to thy bones. Honour The Lord with thy substance, and with the firstfruits of

all thine increase: So shall thy barns be filled with plenty, and thy presses shall burst out with new wine".

I need my Readers to Understand that we can be A Child of God and still Fail and must Fail, because Failure is a part of our Process, to birth within us The Spiritual Discovery to know that without Relationship with our God, we will continue to Fail. It will then be realized that just going to Church is not good enough; we will realize that it takes more than just being a part of the Choir; we will discover that Relationship with God goes way beyond Giving our Tithes and Offerings; it takes more than just a mouth confession. It now Requires an everyday Living and Being What God Requires for us to Be.

With God in the Vessel we can smile at the Storms.

Let Us Pray...

Father of Heaven and Earth, we Honor Your Name; there is no god that can be compared to You; Thou O God, Is Expressed by all Generations from Beginning to Ending to Be Faithful to all who Trust in Thee; Thy Power is Infinite, there is no searching of Your Limitless Understanding; Your Knowledge Is past finding out; Your Wisdom Confuses all those who are wise upon the Earth combined. Father, We come before Your Presence, in no other Name but The Name of Jesus Christ, which Is The Only Access for Man to Reach The Father. Lord we Ask that You Will Forgive us of our Past Transgressions of not being able to Acknowledge You in everything that we would seek to accomplish; Lord Jesus Christ, we ask that You Will Forgive us of Present Transgressions, those that we are aware of, and those that we are not aware of; we Pray In The Name of Jesus Christ, that You will Have us to become Knowledgeable of every Faults that is within our Vessel, that will seek to bring forth a Separation within our Relationship with You.

Father of Heaven, we Pray that You Will Forgive us of Future Transgressions, even those that our Children would have Committed before Your Face. Lord we Pray for Relationship with You, that it will remain Strong, so that we may be able to Overcome every Negative effects of all Opportunities that will come our Direction. Lord, Thou Art The Only Wise God, therefore, we Lean upon Your Understanding to See us through every Challenges that life will Bring. Lord Jesus Christ, it is Clear as day, that Your People will Never be able to lead our own lives, therefore, we Ask in The Name of Jesus Christ that You Will Take Control over every Direction and Decisions that our lives must Travel; Lord we Surrender to Your Will Being Done In Our Lives, this we Pray in The Matchless Name Of Jesus Christ, Amen.

To God Be All The Glory, Great and Mighty Things He Has Done. I Hope this Message would have Inspired God's People, in The Mighty Name of Jesus Christ. From The Ministry of The Church of Jesus Christ Fellowship, Savannah Cross, May Pen, Clarendon, Jamaica, West Indies. From Pastor Lerone Dinnall. God's Blessings Always In The Name of Jesus Christ, Amen.

Take Each Step Of Life Knowing The Face Of The Devil, To Enable Yourself To Be An Overcomer.

HOW TO OVERCOME THE ASSIGNED DEMONS...

Message # 122   Date Started May 7, 2019
                                 Date Finalized May 7, 2019.

Genesis Chapter 3:14-15.

"And The Lord God Said unto the serpent, Because thou hast done this, thou art cursed above all cattle, and above every beast of the field; upon thy belly shalt thou go, and dust shalt thou eat all the days of thy life: And I Will Put enmity between thee and the woman, and between thy seed and her seed; it shall bruise thy head, and thou shalt bruise his heel".

Let's Begin With Prayer...

Most Righteous Eternal Father I approach Your Everlasting Spirit through the only Access Name of Jesus Christ. Father, Thou Art The God of our Forefathers, Namely Abraham, Isaac and Israel; Lord, Thou Art Most Important The God of Covenant. I Ask Father that You Will Continue to Grant the Access of Sins being forgiven over the lives of Your People and especially over the life of Your Servant, has I through Obedience to Your Will Stand as a Mediator for those who does not have the strength to Declare and to Decree that which is our Birthright. Father, as we approach a Topic of this delicacy, I pray

that You Will Reveal all the Ingredients that Your People will need to know to be conquerors over every plan of the enemy. Father, we continue to depend upon Your Love for our lives and we move Boldly into all Purpose that is structured for our lives to be fulfilled in Your Blueprint. Father, we ask that Your Eternal Presence Will Continue to Guide Your People on this Christian's Journey, in The Matchless Name of Jesus Christ we pray, Amen.

I Greet all My Father's Children in The Matchless Name of Jesus Christ, again this is a Privilege to be in this Position that The Lord Can Use me to be of some Inspiration to His Children. There are many Battles we face and must face that we are structured to lose because we have not found ourselves to become discipline to first **KNOW** and Then to **DO** that which The Spirit of God would have Taught us to know what to Do and how to do what we are now Trained to Do when it is that we are attacked by Demons. I used the word Attack because whenever a Demon or Demons comes around our surroundings, it never to wave at us and ask us how are we doing, but rather, Demons are assigned to fulfill deadly acts, with the mission only being to tear down every Spiritual wall that a Child of God has built up for the defense of their soul.

The Lord Revealed to me that it is of utmost importance for a Child of God to **CEMENT** The Spiritual part of their lives 100% in The Unknown Manifestation of The Almighty God; failure to do this will result in a breach of The Spiritual Connection between that Child of God and The Relationship that they have with their Father. The Lord Reveals that if The Spiritual Wall is Torn Down, then Physical life is Shattered, thus a Child of God will have no strength Spiritually or Physically to fulfill the Purpose that is destined over their lives.

The Lord Reveals that every Attack from Demons towards the lives of His People will leave a Scar, there will be some evidence to look back on to remind a believer of what took place in their lives at a fixed time in their lives; The Lord Reveals that this Scar is not a default in The Ability of God to Protect His Children, but rather, it is a part of the Journey for Children of God to Become and Remain to Be Sons of God. The Lord Reveals that during the attack of demons upon the lives of His Children that Spiritual Focus is now very Important, in this experience a Child of God must be Focused on their own Purpose for The Manifestation of God's Kingdom, and while a Child of God Remains Focused on The Promises and on the Duties that are assigned for them to fulfill by The Will of Almighty God, then that Child of God will now discover that all they are going through in that fixed time is just a passing Storm, it will blow away and remove things but The Soul that is Fixed in The Unknown, on The Solid Rock can never be Moved.

The Lord Reveals that when Demons are assigned to Children of God it is a challenge of Dictatorship, the Soul that is equipped with The Foundation of The Word of God will be The Child of God that will Overcome any Assigned Demons. The Spiritual Mind and Will of a Child of God has got to be and remain being strong and be already prepared to look Demons in The Eyes if it is that they are being manifested within a person, you have to look those demons in the eye and now Declare and Decree what you now desire for the environment of your life to be. If it is that your faced with demons that comes in spirit or spirits, then within that atmosphere that the spirits have now created, a Child of God must now be forceful to Dictate what shall be and what shall not be according to The Measurement of The Holy Ghost that is Manifesting in the life of that Child of God. If The Child of God cannot exercise their Birthright to now Declare and Decree, then that Child of God will become a puppet, that which the demon or demons have now dictated what they were assigned to fulfill and even worse to happen in the life of that Child of God.

We are The Temple of God, it's not a Building! The Temple of God Walks, Sleeps, Works, Worship, Praise, Marries and Grows a Family for God's Inheritance, thus resulting in a continual supply of Sons of God for God's Glory. If The Souls of The Temple of God cannot be activated to let The Holy Ghost

Protect The Temple, then how will The Spirit of God Live to Manifest in that Temple? _____

_____.

There are times that whatever is assigned for a Child of God to face it becomes so overwhelming, that it would seem that there is no more Spiritual Strength, if that Child of God is found on The Foundation of God's Word, then that Child of God can actually begin to tease that demon or demons to fulfill that which they have been sent to do.

Because demons are mainly assigned to create an environment that will cause a spirit of fear to be developed by us who are of The Foundation of a Child of God, but they have no power to remove us from The Foundation, therefore while the fear of the now fixed environment is seeking to choke the very confidence from our Souls, TRUTH must be Manifested within the Soul of that Child of God to know that if the devil was given the permission by God to take away our lives, then that's what he would have immediately come and do, he would not be Delaying that assignment to spend it speaking to our soul to bring forth fear, he would immediately kill us because Purpose from our lives for God's Kingdom is what he is fixed to stop.

The Lord Reveals that there are many of His Children that have not yet found their Spiritual Voice to Speak back to Demons and spirits that are plaguing their lives, because we have not yet understood what is TRUTH. There are some of God's Children that need to first Believe that they are a Child of The King and become knowledgeable of their Birthright, which was, which is and always will be to Declare and Decree what is in The Mind of God.

Genesis Chapter 1:1-3.

"In The Beginning God Created the Heaven and the Earth. And the Earth was without form, and void; and darkness was upon the face of the deep. And The

Spirit of God Moved upon the face of the waters. And God Said, Let there be Light: and there was light".

There is no fixed situation that God's Children will face that our Father has not already Given unto us The Ability to dig down deep within to find The Same Anointing that was used in the beginning, to now open our mouth with confidence and Declare and Decree to every demons, spirits, environment, fixed condition, that your time is up, because, if you were given the permission to take away my life, you're so evil and envious that I know that if it was spoken out of The Mouth of God that it is my time to pass from this life to the other, I know the devil will not spare me for a day or even a second because he is mindful of my purpose for God.

A Personal Declaration...

I speak to all demons and spirits, if you can't fulfill your mission and your threats, I Declare and Decree from The Foundation of The Holy Ghost that the darkest part of my life is now over, and I Declare and Decree that it's The Breaking of The day for my life, my family, and The Ministry that God Has Given me, In The Almighty Name Of Jesus Christ, Amen.

Psalms 118:17.

"I Shall not die, but live, and DECLARE The Work of The Lord".

From The Ministry of The Church of Jesus Christ Fellowship, Savannah Cross, May Pen, Clarendon, Jamaica, West Indies, to God Be All Glory, Honor and Praise from Beginning to Eternity, God Bless. From Pastor Lerone Dinnall.

Your Focus For God's Purpose Within Your Life Will Be Your Strength...

WHO WAS LUCIFER... AND WHO IS LUCIFER NOW?

Message # 36   **Date Started July 3, 2016**
Date Finalized July 3, 2016.

How can I say thanks, for things you've done for me; things so undeserved; I feel so special that God has Saved my Soul. I Greet the Family of God, in The Name of Jesus Christ, our soon coming King. WOW! I never thought that I would have seen a topic like this. But here it is, and am excited to see what The Lord Is Going to Reveal through this Topic. The Lord Gave me a topic a while back; it went like this:

> **"Study your weaknesses in order to overcome**
> **that weakness; he that knoweth not his weakness**
> **will continue to be overcomed by it"**!

This was a personal message to me from God; in order for me to be stronger. I made mention of that topic because we are now in discussion with this topic. I don't know about you; I know the manifestation of who Lucifer is present is not a good image; therefore, I'm dying to find out what were his characteristics developed from who he was to who he is right now that caused him to become the Devil he is now today. Because, I believe that if I can do a study on that which caused him to fail; then I believe that I can look within myself to make sure that the evidence of these characteristics are not found in me, or not given the type of spiritual feeding to manifest those characteristics. And if there is some evidence of these characteristics in me or in us; then we both have a lot of Fasting and Prayers to do to ensure that we get rid of these faults. Let us first understand that God, The Father of The Universe, He made all things Perfect; with the main purpose that everything that He had Made should Please Him. What happened to Lucifer you may ask?.

I declared some Facts in previous topics that Lucifer manifested the mother of all sins which is called **INIQUITY** which births a spirit of **ENVY**; which became a Seed of **ENVY**; that grew, and consumed his whole mind, letting him believe that, that which he taught by the evidence of the Seed **ENVY**, he would have been able to bring it to pass. Talk about your bubble being burst; The Bible along with other books declared that Lucifer never even got the chance to carry out his plans; because The Lord that Rules both Spiritual and Physical, Saw Inside The Spiritual exactly what was in the mind of Lucifer. The Lord called upon Michael the Archangel; and gave him this Word:

"Go Tell Lucifer, THE LORD REBUKE HIM"!

Only that Word from God was needed; and immediately Lucifer and all those who were influenced by him, had to flee from The Presence of The Divine Spirituality of The Lord. That was not the only punishment, his position was completely removed, it was like it never existed, to be seen no more.

Lord, please keep me **HUMBLE AT YOUR FEET** .

Let us seek to understand more about the topic. You must realize that the Topic has two parts. The first part being:

Who Was Lucifer…

Let us find the answer. I want my readers to understand that we are not looking for the easiest answer; but instead, we are going to give an explanation of what God Made Lucifer to be, what his job was, his purpose and his position.

The name and the person Lucifer; according to The Bible Dictionary, he was known as the SHINING ONE; THE MORNING STAR. According to The Bible he was known as the SON OF THE MORNING; the one that weakens nations. Isaiah Chapter 14:12-16. According to Bible Aids; he was known as GOD'S RIGHT HAND MAN. Some Bible Aid have it to say that Lucifer was the chief Angel that brought the other Angels into Worshiping for God. It also gives the expression that there was no other Angel that had a higher ranking than him. Only GOD THE FATHER that Created him was The Highest Above Lucifer, Looking down on everything and Ruleth All Things and Receiveth The Glory and Praise from all things that He, The Father Has Created. And for this Position of God, Lucifer developed Iniquity against God, which birth the spirit and seed of ENVY. **Who Was Lucifer...** This was what he was. When I consider all this evidence; I began to examine myself carefully; because I have now realized that it is not to get on top of the mountain; it's not to be the very best above everyone else; it's not to be the greatest that ever walked the face of the earth. It is more necessary to know that every position that God Places us in; we need to get up each day, and ask God to please help us to remain **HUMBLE and magnify the position that God Has Breath upon us to execute.** Because at the end of the day, no one is going to remember us without the fulfillment of our destined Position from our Father. if we didn't finish the race; it would all be **VAIN.** Let us look at ourselves now, our Family; that person who we are now; Saved and Sanctified; is this the same person we're going to be at the end of the race? BIG; BIG QUESTION?

And Who Is Lucifer Now?

The Bible Dictionary says that Lucifer now, is the Archangel that was hurled from Heaven, for his wickedness. The Webster's Dictionary says: Lucifer is a PROUD REBELLIOUS Archangel, identified as Satan, who fell from Heaven. The Bible describes Lucifer as being so PROUD that he never believed that he could be brought down to the grave. Let me share with you a reading from the Secrets of Enoch; coming from The Lost Book of The Bible.

Chapter 29:3-4. GOD Was Speaking To Enoch Said:

"And one from out the order of Angels, having turned away with the order that was under him, conceived an impossible thought, to place his throne higher than the clouds above the earth, that he might become equal in rank to my power. And I threw him out from the height with his angels, and he was flying in the air continuously above the bottomless".

The Bible Says in Isaiah Chapter 14:12-16. Lucifer said in his heart, I will ascend into Heaven, I will exalt my throne above the stars of GOD: I will sit also upon the mount of the congregation, in the sides of the north: I will ascend above the heights of the clouds; and here is the big evidence of INIQUITY which births the spirit and Seed of ENVY: Finally Lucifer said I will be like **THE MOST HIGH**. Do you now realize the pattern with the spirit of INIQUITY which births the Seed of ENVY. These were the same exact words that the Serpent in the garden used to influence Eve to eat of the fruit that was forbidden for herself and Adam to eat. The Serpent said to Eve:

"For God doth know that in the day ye eat thereof, then your eyes shall be opened, and ye shall be as gods, knowing good and evil". Genesis Chapter 3.

Eve and then Adam; not that they didn't remember what God Commanded them; but INIQUITY was formed and ENVY was birth, thus the Seed of ENVY consumed their minds to think, just as how Lucifer taught, that there was even a possibility that they can measure up to be like God.

The spirit and seed of ENVY is the First Child that is born from the Mother of all Sin, which is INIQUITY otherwise known to us as Disobedience to God's Commandment. The fact is, before Eve and then Adam Sinned, God Already Knew In The Spiritual that they would have sinned because they weren't really the main plan for God's Kingdom Building, but for the direction of choice and freewill, man had to pave their own destiny even though it is already written in The Mind of God. From this Sin of INIQUITY or Disobedient cometh all other Sin. Adam and Eve LUSTED; DESIRED AND BURNED WITH ENVY, just like Lucifer; who wanted to be like God. They also wanted to be like God; not knowing that God had already made them to be the god of the earth; having the authority to have access to command everything on the earth; because of THE MIND OF GOD that was in them. In The Bible Aids, it expresses that when the Angels saw Adam and Eve; they bowed down before them, because of the GLORY that God had placed upon them.

Examining the Sin of Lucifer's Heart; it made me realize that, when it is that we spend so much time considering how we are going to reach the next level. We should have been spending a lot more time in The Word of the Lord; and then we would have realized that The Word of God Says:

"My Glory Will I Not Give To Another. The Word of God Says: I Sit on the Pinnacle of everything, and I Only Look Down; because there is nothing Above Me"!

If we are spending most of our time in The Word of God; then it is a must; we will know about God; therefore allowing us not to make the same mistake that Lucifer made. Now because Lucifer lost every-thing; that which he had; and that which he taught he could have achieved. The Bible Said that there is no place of Repentance for him. Therefore the mind and the heart of Lucifer is fixed to ensure that, he does all in his power to prevent those of us on the earth, who believe and is working towards getting to Heaven; because he knows the Glory and the Splendors of Heaven; and also knows that he will never be able to see it again; because his position and office is taken away by God for all Eternity.

Each day we awake people of God; just expect a fight. Don't wake up for one morning thinking that ourselves and Lucifer are friends; therefore, thinking that he's not going to give us a hard time. When we expect a fight; we will prepare ourselves for it. Don't worry people of God; as long as we are FAITHFUL TO GOD; He Promises that He Will Never Leave us nor Forsake us.

I get up in the Morning, and have my Devotion; before I leave the house, I repeat these words:

> **"ONE MORE DAY; ONE MORE CHALLENGE; WHICH MEANS ONE MORE VICTORY: BY THEE HAVE I RUN THROUGH A TROOP; AND BY MY GOD, HAVE I LEAPED OVER A WALL IN THE NAME OF JESUS CHRIST, AMEN"!**

The Bible illustrated Handbook describes Lucifer as being **100% ARROGANT.** Now I need the people of God to take a look at some of the characteristics of Lucifer; the number one fault that came out was the word PROUD; which is PRIDE. If you recall in The Bible; being Proud is the first thing out of a list of seven that God Hates. The meaning of the word Arrogant says: Offensive display of superiority or Self-importance; Overbearing Pride; Haughtiness. Now when you add a spirit of Pride along with a spirit of Arrogance; and put with that also a spirit of a LYING TONGUE; this definitely is a mixture that will explode in the Nostril of God as Unworthy for Acceptance. A lying tongue is the Second item in the list of seven that God Hates.

A topic came to me recently that says:

"To Re-Measure yourself to see if that which you say you are; that's who you really are"!

I haven't written anything as yet concerning this topic; but upon looking at this topic that we are exploring; I realize why God wanted me to look at this topic. What if! What if! What if I say that I'm a Bishop; or a Pastor; an Evangelist; a Priest; a Prophet; I Declare that I'm God's Eyes and Hears on earth; and at the same time on God's Scale, God's Measurement Reads: **ARROGANCE**; it reads **PROUD**; it reads that I have a **LYING TONGUE!** Ask yourself WHAT IF. Would I not find myself being in the same position that Lucifer found himself in?

Therefore, no one needs to call me Brother Dinnall; or Deacon Dinnall; or Minister Dinnall; or Pastor Dinnall; or Overseer Dinnall; or Bishop Dinnall. According to The Word of God; whatever spirits it is that governs a man; that man is now sealed by the spirit that governs him. Therefore, we can forget about the title and the name that we have; we can automatically call ourselves Lucifer; because the same spirit that governs Lucifer; that made him who he is from who he was originally; that's the same spirit that is now in full effect in our lives, if we have moved away from The Pure Discipline of God's Way .

I didn't say that we should go around and call anyone by the name Lucifer. I'm just asking us to make sure that the first person we Judge; let it be the man that we see in the mirror when we look in it. All over the world there are Saints that are becoming better Christians; what say me and you. One of my clients, who is a Christian, told me recently that she heard the voice of the Lord telling her to speak to her Church Family, that The Lord Said:

"LET THE CHURCH BE THE CHURCH".

The Trumpet of The Lord is about to Sound; the Dead in Christ is about to Raise; are we in a position that is known as **READY WAITING**. If not, there is still a lot of work to do; and the time to start is NOW.

Who Was Lucifer... And Who Is Lucifer Now ? I would like to share with you a story that an Evangelist told the Church a long time ago. This story never leaves me; because always, I want to make sure that my Salvation is on the right track. The Evangelist said that there was a young man in the Church that started off very well; you could see the evidence of God's Glory all over his life; and knew that he was doing what God Required of him to do. The Evangelist said that this was a Church that she visited; therefore she had to leave because she was just passing by.

She said that she again traveled to that country, about Six years after; and went back to the same Church. This time she was inquiring about the young man that she saw six years before; she came to a certain brother in the Church and asked him; where is the Brother that was always shouting and speaking in tongues; prophesying and preaching God's Word. She said to the young man; could you tell me what happened to him; if he migrated or is going to another Church? The young man surprisingly answered the Evangelist; and told her that the young man that she was looking for was he. The same person that she was speaking to. She Expressed to us that she could not believe it; reason being, that which he was six years ago; is a great transformation of who he is, six years after. And she was not speaking of him being better; but being worse, that she could not even recognize that he was that person. It was so bad that The Glory of God was no longer a part of his life. I never forgot that story, I would never desire that experience on any Child of God. I shared this testimony so that there can be a direct reflection of that which the topic is expressing.

The Start of our Salvation is Good and Important; but what makes our Salvation counts, is the finish line. Everyone Starts, but how

many of those who started actually finished the journey? _____
_____. Here Is A Question:
Will I finish the race?_____.

Lucifer was made Perfect; with Holy and Righteous Calling, with Purpose and Position. He chose to change from the Purpose God made him for; and he's no longer the Bright Morning Star; he's now in the Darkest Pit of Hell; having no light. There is a king in the Bible that had the same Arrogant and Proud spirit that is displayed in Lucifer. The King was Nebuchadnezzar, King of Babylon. This King, even though he was warned by a dream, which was later interpreted by Daniel, of what was going to happen to him. With Pride and Arrogance; he declared out of his mouth that the kingdom which he ruleth, was built by his own hands; by his own power and for the honor of his majesty. The Bible Said that while the King was still speaking; The Word of The Lord came from Heaven and Rebuked him; and cursed him for a season; until he recognize that it was God The Almighty that caused him to achieve; that caused him to build; that caused him to rule and to be king; that caused him to change into an animal to that of a cow; and eat the food of a cow; to be treated like a beast of the field; it was God that turned him back into a man; it was God that place him back on his throne in his kingdom, which he had given him; for him to rule again. God Taught Nebuchadnezzar a valuable lesson; of how not to be PROUD, and not be ARROGANT. The King Learned HUMILITY the hard way. The story can be found in Daniel Chapter 4. In my Bible the story is known as the King's Prideful Boast. These things are written for our examples, to let us know if there is ever a spirit of Pride and Arrogance in us or any other spirits. Then God has the cure to calm every rough sea. In completing this Message, I would like to leave with you a word from the illustrated Bible Handbook, concerning Lucifer and his actions.

"Whatever you decide after reading about the characteristics of Lucifer; the application of this message is clear. Every

Arrogance which exalts itself against God, in Satan, in Kings, or in you and me, will fall under judgment".

From The Ministry of The Church of Jesus Christ Fellowship, Savannah Cross, May Pen, Clarendon, Jamaica, West Indies. From The Servant of God, Pastor Lerone Dinnall. God Bless You Always In The Name of Jesus Christ, Amen.

Who Was Lucifer... And Who Is Lucifer Now?

The Sin That We Do…
That We Know Not What We Do…

INIQUITY…

Message # 12

Date Started May 31, 2016
Date Finished June 12, 2016.

Greetings to all the Wonderful Family of God, in The Matchless Name of Jesus Christ our Soon Coming King. I count this Opportunity once more as a Great privilege to be in a position of writing for you another Message Inspired by The Lord Our Saviour and Friend.

A Question was asked to a person on a particular day; and that question was: If someone knew what your future holds; and that person was able to tell you when you were going to die; would you, being the receiver of that Message, want to receive such information?
_____

Think about it, would you?_____. The reason for starting off the Message like this is to create an atmosphere within our Mind; Body and Soul; to allow us all to put great emphasis on that which we call our Soul. To put the Question that was asked in a different light; let's say I'm looking at myself; and it is a Fact that I've been Serving God for the past thirty (30) years; now according to my own judgment of how I've been Serving God, maybe I would give myself a pass mark; because it is then that I will be looking Physically on all that I've been doing; being an active member in the Church; a person that miss only a few Service at Church; it's a possibility that my Mind will sway to the point to remember that I'm excellent in offering my Tithes; I would also remember that I also love to give an healthy Offering; I give to those who are in need; then after considering all these positives; I would look on myself and smile; in that very Moment I would have put myself in The Position of God; to Judge for myself that, I Pastor Dinnall is doing all that is required to bring pleasure to The Father of All Things; not knowing that I may have just allowed myself to be like the Pharisee that went into The House of God to pray, along with the publican; we know the story: The Pharisee was full of Pride and only looked on that which he was doing; and in the process missed what he should be doing in that moment of time.

We are all guilty of this action of the mind to muse in the Spiritual, to think of and about something that should never have received the birth of that imagination. We at times take great pride in that which we know that we are doing for God. But the little thing and most important thing that we were not considering, is that which we were not doing for our Father, considering that we were already Anointed by God to fulfill that which we were Destined by God to fulfill. How many times do we look within ourselves and say yes, I know that I'm already doing this for God, let's now elevate to another level to do that which I'm not yet doing for God in agreement to that which is God's Will for our lives. And to have a Mind like this starts with Humility.

The thing that we need to consider is that, that which we are doing for God; has now reach a point in our lives that it is now perfect; thus leaving a gap to take on other things as a challenge, for those things to now become perfect; we must always seek to continue Improving in God. I heard a Testimony recently; the Sister said that she received a vision from God; and it was seen through her eyes in the vision that God was gathering His People for the Rapture; the Sister Testified and said, that The Lord looked on her while she was in her white robe, preparing to enter the Marriage; she said, that The Lord Said to her that she must look on her robe that she was wearing, because there was some spots on her garment; she said that she looked for herself, and did not see any spots; The Lord Told her to look again; she looked, but still did not see any spots; The Lord Told her to look the third time; she said when she looked, it was now visible;

she saw the spots The Lord was Talking about. She said that The Lord Told her that she needed to correct these spots that were on her garment, because there is no way she will be able to enter Heaven with a garment that has Spots. When I heard this testimony, I knew that this was a True Report; if you look at what the Sister revealed in her Testimony; you would also identify that there is no way she would have made up something like that; especially something that made her feel bad. The Sister said that she looked, but did not see what God was Seeing. It took her three times to look, before it was Revealed to her what was really wrong.

I gave a question earlier which allowed us to realize that if we ever leave it up to ourselves to Judge our own selves; then we will no doubt find ourselves in the position that no matter how much we look at ourselves; all we would basically see are the things that we are doing right. We will never stop to examine the things that we are doing wrong; and try to work on those wrongs so that they will become a part of the right. I tell you the Truth; if we should do a Survey now; majority of Christians will not even identify the things that we are doing wrong; but we can definitely tell all that we are doing right. Here is an example Christians; this of the Man Christ that we seek to replicate to please God: Have you ever read anywhere in the Gospel, about the Ministry of Christ, that someone or any-one heard Him Speaking about what He was doing Right! Have you ever read anywhere in the Gospel, Christ was Speaking about what He had Accomplished to make Himself look good! The answer is no. That is the reason why He is our Perfect Example. Christ was always seen Crying; Praying; Healing the sick; Working Miracles; having the desire to go and do the next Mission; and never once did He required any Glory; Recognition; Rewards for that which God Allowed Him to Accomplish; He even said that if He bares record of Himself, is record is not true. This He said to let us know that He did not come to be Recognized by man; but instead to Please only God. It is full time that we all get to realize that as Christ came to Fulfill The Will of His Father; so are we all Called to Fulfill The Will of God Almighty; not expecting any Rewards or Recognition from man to do what God Needs us to Do.

To know the Destiny of one's life; if you think very hard about it you will recognize that the BIBLE itself is Teaching us about our Destiny. Also letting us know that we all have a choice to ensure that we obtain the Right Future by a word that is called **FREE WILL.** The Topic says, "The Things That We Do… That We Know Not What We Do… INIQUITY". We have already identified one of the main things that Manifest Iniquity; and that is not recognizing what we are establishing within the spiritual of our Minds that which is wrong; but to think that we are doing so many things right by the same manifestation of our Minds to believe that what we have imagined it must be right even if it moves away from The Will and Direction of our Father.

Another thing to identify is that, there are so many things that we are doing that God did not necessarily Asked us to do those things; but indeed we took it upon ourselves to do those things, because we've identified someone else doing those things and think within ourselves that if we are able to do those things it will make our Resume look a lot better to enter Heaven. Things that we've discovered other Saints doing; think! If it is that God had Commanded them to Do it, they will receive their Reward. But if someone outside of the portfolio of that Anointing takes it upon themselves to do something that other Saints have found themselves manifesting for God because that's their calling, then the person who is performing the spirits of patterning has no rewards to receive from God.

For some of us, all God Asked for us to Do is to come and Follow Him. Yes! Following does include movement of that which is required to perform for God, but some movement from The Direction of our Father requires special training and a greater level of God's Anointing to execute that which is required from God perfectly. According to the Revelation through this Message it clearly establishes Iniquity as something that we do that we at times have no knowledge that we have committed a Sin within The Spiritual that expresses a sure offering to The Sovereign God. This brings to Mind that Iniquity is indeed a Spiritual Sin and the first of all Sins that is to be committed by man, this is established within the spiritual part of a man, when speaking about the spiritual part of a man, we're basically identifying the debts of the Mind and the Heart. The Mind is The Spiritual foundation of everything to come into existence, the Heart is the physical expression of that which the mind has already formed or given life to.

The Bible would have for us to know that God Recognizes Iniquity within the Mind and Heart of an Individual; without you and me the person in question actually identifying for ourselves that, that which we are thinking is not really a secret, it may present itself to us being a secret but to our Father, Lord and King, there is no secrets that can hide in the spiritual where God is Complete Master and Lord. Isaiah Chapter 14:10-16. Psalms 66:18. This Topic should make us realize that if we cannot **Think** Good of an Individual; then don't think anything at all; because there is a God that is Firm within The Spiritual that Moves, Sees; Hears; Smells; Feels; Understands, has the Knowledge of and Measures everything with Divine Wisdom of what man establishes to ensure that it is Justified in His Eyes for the rewards that is to be executed for that man.

I will share with you a story that recently came my way. Someone called me about a month ago, and began to share with me a vision that they had concerning my life; by the time the person finished speaking; you would have thought that the person was a Prophet, or a person that goes around and Warns People. I Thank God for the Instructions My Bishop gave to me; and that's the Instruction of how to filter out Messages that comes with the Intention of Destroying our Soul; also known as **BAD SEEDS**. Bishop Austin Whitfield would say:

"Words that are spoken directly to him with Bad Intentions being Bad Seeds; he only allows it to pass from one Ear to

the other Ear; by doing this, it allows for that Bad Seed not to take Root in his Spirit, to affect his Spiritual Growth".

When I think about it, and consider that this is not the first person to say something bad about my life; but the Reality of it is, that GOD Always has the Final Say… When I look back to consider I Realize that all that have stood before me to Condemn my life; two things have happened to those who spoke those words:

1. **That which they have Predicted for my life, happened to them, instead of me.**
2. **They are now dead or so far away that I don't see them anymore.**

I've been trying to understand the process of Message delivery from God, the sad thing is, that for many that are delivering messages have not yet come to the full understanding of the process to deliver a word. There are many that have not yet identified that if a Message or a word is being delivered to A Child that is Serving The Living God, then when that Word has been delivered it will be in the form of a Conformation to the Child of God and not to reflect a Spirit within a Child of God that will see this Child of God Rejecting that which is being spoken to the Soul. How is it that a person that is so Messed up in their life, even think that God can Give them a Message for someone's life; some people go as for as to give you Advice, to let you know how you can fix your life or how you can become a better Christian or Employee. That Advice did not seem to pass their direction to let them know that they should try and fix themselves first. St Matthew Chapter 7:1. Says:

"Judge not, that ye be not judge".

When I truly consider it, Messages of Warnings; should I not try to ask God what is wrong with me that I can fix myself? If God is going to Give me a word to give to someone else, so that their lives can be better; should not The God that Loves His Children, Give a word to me first; so that I can Fix myself! It is my belief that when I am now Fixed or received my Word from God and walking Upright before God that others can see that I'm Walking; then and only then can I be Given the Approval to Instruct someone else with their problem. The Bible Asked us to take the **BEAM** out of our eyes first; then we can see clearly to take the **MOTE** out of our brother's eye. This Example my Readers, given from one person to another under the guise of being Instructions to help is one of the Greatest formations of the spirit of **INIQUITY.** Another formation of INIQUITY rests within the Mind and Heart of people, what we Think or Believe about a person in an evil manner. Now these are the people or saints that will never get an Answer from God, because The Bible Says:

"If I regard INIQUITY in my Heart
The Lord will not Hear me".

The Lord Reminded me everytime that I take The Bible to Preach, and His Words are always the same:

"The Words spoken by the preacher is for that preacher first, then it journeys to those who will now hear those words"!

Many people have it to say that I don't listen to people! Can you blame me; all that people have to say to you is something Discouraging, nothing that is Seasoned with Grace; nothing that speaks towards Edifying and to give Life. The main evidence is manifested in The Response of The Holy Ghost that lives in A Child of God's Vessel. The Holy Ghost is never wrong because it Represents The Eternal Spirit of Life and it's Main Responsibility for A Child of God is to Protect the Temple. I found out that many people are of the Mindset that, if their own life is not going anywhere, neither should the life of others be going somewhere. In Jamaica it is known as **Crabs in a Barrel Mentality**. No matter how hard one Crab tries to rise above, to get out of that Barrel, there will always be another Crab trying to pull him down back; and the Cycle continues and continues; and by the time we Realize what is going on, Forty years (40) has passed and we still haven't Reached close to our Destination.

My Advice to my Readers, try to follow the Example of Christ; we've never read that Jesus Christ took Advice from any person; He Said:

"I Came To Do The Will Of My Father".

When He needed Advice He went up to the Mountain to Pray; and that was where He got His Advice; Divine Advice that could not Fail. There was one occasion that Peter gave Advice to Jesus Christ, that Advice ended with a **REBUKE**; because it was not in The WILL of God to Accept an Advice like that. So even though you're reading this Message, and it is indeed an Advice on a particular Topic; if you realize within your spirit that this Message is giving you wrong Instructions or Advice, you have the permission of myself and that of God to stop reading this Message. As I told the members in the Church, if you come to Church and believe that the Pastor is not leading you in The Will of God; then it is your Responsibility to find a Church that will Lead you to Christ. The Point I'm trying to make is that we have got to be VERY CAREFUL of our Salvation; in many ways we just have One Opportunity to do what is Right, as it was the Example of Adam and Eve.

For The People of God that knows for sure that they have a Spiritual Flow that is indeed leading their lives, be careful of who and where advice is coming from. If the advice is coming from someone that does not understand nor have experienced what it is like to have The Divine Spiritual Flow from God over a person's life, then that advice whoever and wherever it is coming from cannot help a Child of God that is experiencing The Spiritual Divine Flow of The Father.

You Are Warned!

We cannot allow anyone to prevent us from reaching our Goal. Here is one thing that we need to recognize about the Judgment:

"Ye did run well, but who did hinder thee from obeying the truth; depart from me I know you not".

There are some of us that don't like to hear that part of the Scripture, but I love to read it, because it acts as a constant reminder of what I should be doing to make it into God's Kingdom. It makes me Realize that Friends cannot help; Money cannot help, Wife cannot help, Children cannot help. The only thing on this Earth that can help me is **THE ENGRAFTED WORDS OF GOD** which is able to Save my Soul. Apart from the Words of God; I am the only person that can help myself; this I have to be willing to Accept.

I'm hungry to see **TRUE SAINTS OF GOD** that will not Dilute what God Ask of them to Do; I'm hungry to see Saints that are trying their very best to do The Will of God comes what may. But everywhere I look, it is sad to say, there are only a few True Worshippers; and those who you're Training seem to not be able to Grasp the Understanding to know what is Expected of them. I wonder if after reading this Message we will get a Commitment of a Covenant between those of us who are Christians unto God, to establish a Promise with God that we are going to Do more than our best to ensure that we Do His Will; we are going to Elevate to another level and start to recognize those things which we are not doing for God, to begin a purposeful diet of doing them within The Leading of The Almighty Father.

I think that is what God Needs from us; A New Covenant; A New Beginning; A New Purpose for living; I think that's the reason for this Message; that we can be Aware of those Sin that we do… That we know not what we do… which is **INIQUITY**. Now that we are Aware of what Iniquity is; we will now be in a better Position to Do what God Requires us to Do. Thank you for Reading this Message, I hope that this Message was a Blessing to you; Let us all seek to find out those Faults that we have, in order to correct them; or else we won't be able to Enter The Kingdom of God because of **INIQUITY**. In The Matchless Name of Jesus Christ Our Soon Coming King. From your Faithful Servant; Pastor Lerone Dinnall. God Bless.

The Sin That We Do...
That We Know Not What We Do...

INIQUITY!

IF WE FAIL TO STAND IN POSITION, WE WILL PERMANENTLY LOSE OUR POSSESSION.

Message # 119
Date Started March 31, 2019
Date Finalized March 31, 2019.

Loving Father, Prince of Peace, Savior Jesus Christ; I Give All Honor and Praise to Your Eternal Spirit. Blessed and Highly Favored am I to again be in this Position, humble and willing to do what God Would have me to do, I must remain for His Glory to be Fulfilled.

To Understand is a Spirit that God Has Granted for His Children to Move in the capacity of that Understanding. There are many times because of a lack of understanding God's People lose that which is for their Benefit because we are not aware of our **POSITION** that God Has Granted for us to stand in. We are Destroyed The Bible Says for a lack of Knowledge. Hosea Chapter 4:6.

Let's begin in The Spiritual before looking at The Physical: Lucifer, known as The Son of the Morning, was given the Position to gather the Angels into worship before God, this Position he moved away from, and now desired through the manifestation of Iniquity which births Envy, of seeking to establish his kingdom above The Most

High God. The explanation of Lucifer gathering the Angels into worship before God is not found in The Bible, therefore let no one quote this Message to say I said that The Bible Said. The Bible Remains to be The Basic Instruction Before Leaving Earth, the Question is This: Will God Not Reveal Advance Instructions that has its Foundation still being that of The Holy Book? _____
_____.

The Explanations in other Books with The Foundation of The Bible and The Divine Revelation of God Reveals that Lucifer was set in a Specific Position, but The Manifestation of Iniquity which Births Envy resulted in Lucifer Losing his Position that God Gave to him and also lost the Possession of Heaven forever.

I was Teaching The Church today and explained that for God to Move Lucifer out of his Position forever and cut off his Possession, this manifestation Declare and Decree that God Does Not Love Lucifer because of his Intended Purpose which began with Iniquity that Births Envy. This new purpose of Lucifer was out of Alignment with God's Spiritual Laws which Dictates God's Movements from Spiritual to Physical and Back again to Spiritual that God's Will Must Be Done. And so is it for everyone that follows in the Manifestation of that which Lucifer Established to move from his intended purpose to now desire The One and Only Position of The Most High God. It is Revealed to me by The Spirit of God that whoever God Is In Love with, when they sin and takes a long time to repent, God Knows that they will repent, to thus be renewed in their Rightful Position to Stand Upright before God.

Therefore for God to Bring back a sinner from the claws of Hell to again stand Upright before His Presence, it means that God Never Fell out of Love with those who are destined to be Saved. On The other hand, Lucifer was not Granted that benefit of Repentance because God no longer Loved him because of his new intended purpose of needing to be established above his Creator. Not only was Lucifer Rebuked and Damned from his Position and Possession, but also every angel that came into agreement with the same mind of Iniquity which Physical manifestation is Envy.

Let us have a look at the Physical Manifestation: It is Mentioned in The Bible in The Book of Genesis Chapter two that God Made Man in His Image, it also said that God Instructed the Man of what he must do and what he should not do, because the day in which the man disobeyed God, that man will die. Adam and Eve Position was to be in Command of The Garden of Eden to therefore Obey that which God Instructed for them to fulfill in Alignment with The Words that says: "Let Thy Will Be Done". Eve and Adam Moved out of Position therefore they found themselves into big trouble not only for themselves but for their entire generation. The first thing to understand about this story is to become Knowledgeable that Adam and Eve's Position was not to take Instruction from anyone but God. The Moment Eve and Adam Adopted to a new master, they found themselves temporarily out of Position and Possession. Because of Love from God, God Immediately Exposed The New Way for man to Return to his Rightful Position of being Obedient to only The Voice and Movement of God.

Esau being the first born of Isaac and Rebekah, he sold his birthright to Jacob for a meal not knowing that he was trading away his Position before God, this Position was no longer accessible for the life of Esau and his descendants because it was now in the hand and upon the life of Jacob. The Lord Spoke in The Book of Malachi Chapter 1:2-4.

> **"I have Loved you, Saith The Lord. Yet ye say, wherein hast thou loved us? Was not Esau Jacob's brother? Saith The Lord: Yet I Loved Jacob, and I Hated Esau, and laid his mountains and his heritage waste for the dragons of the wilderness. Whereas Edom saith, We are impoverished, but we will return and build the desolate places; Thus Saith The Lord of Hosts, they shall build, but I Will Throw down; and they shall call them, The Border of wickedness, and, The people against whom The Lord hath Indignation forever".**

The Manifestation of this Scripture Reveals that those who have moved themselves out of the Position that God Has Destined for that person to stand in, now because purpose of God's Will Being Manifested out of that person is destroyed, it now reveals that God is no longer in Love with that person because that person is found to be out of Position for the Manifestation of God's Will Being Done. Therefore being out of Position will Automatically Reveal that such a person is also out of Possession of God's Glory.

This was also identified in the life of king Saul, the moment king Saul moved out of Position to allow for God's Will to be Manifested through his life, that's the very moment God Moved His Anointing from Saul to that of David, because all Position from God Must Reveal God's Will Being Done. Saul Moved out of Position and lost all Possessions for himself and his generation.

I asked The Church a Question today, of which I will also be asking my Readers: What is The Church Position for God?_____
_____.
An Individual going to Church to Serve The Living God, What is our Position for God? _____
_____.
If we have not yet found out what it is that we must stand in for God, then allow this Message to become a wakeup call:

"Let us Find Ourselves In The Position that God Has Placed us to Be In, or else we are going to lose our Possession"!

If we could just stand on the outside of ourselves and view what others are seeing when God is Using us to Manifest His Will Being Done, then we would have finally realized why it is that so many people would desire for us to walk and to step away from The Position that God Has Invested in us to Stand, Walk and Manifest In. We must see God's Position and Duties as a **MUST** and not a maybe or when we feel like doing it. It must be activated within us whenever time The Master Burns us to Move.

There must never be the thought within our minds to think that God Cannot do without us; Wake Up! The story of Elijah reveals to us that God Always Has many in Reserved to do what we are doing and even to fulfill God's Requirements with even more effect than that which we are doing currently. But every Child of God must have their destined time to manifest for The Glory of God's Will Being Done. After all is said and done, we are all working for God's Penny. Let us make certain that the day we spend working for God will manifest a day of **QUALITY** to thus earn our due reward.

Unto The God that Remains Holy unto all Generations, to Him be All Glory, Honor and Praise. From The Ministry of The Church of Jesus Christ Fellowship, Savannah Cross, Jamaica, West Indies. I Know this Message will Inspire and Refuel God's People, God Bless. Pastor Lerone Dinnall.

If Our Position is not Manifesting Our Possession, then it's time to have a look at The Foundation of Our Position.

The Only Position that Leads to Possession Is Jesus Christ.

PHASE TWO

The Body;
The Son of God;
Jesus Christ;
The Direct Divine Link and Only
Access from The Divine
Spiritual to The Physical;
The Divine Mediator;
The Second Adam;
The Second Manifestation or Step from
The Highest Authority of God...

THE AUTHORITY!

Message # 132

Date Started May 14, 2020.
Date Finalized May 15, 2020.

I have seen and I have heard, and that which is Given to me by the use of The GODHEAD I'm asked to write.

Unto The God of Excellent Understanding, Knowledge and Wisdom be all Glory, Honor and Praise. Only Through His Intelligence am I made to be visible, without God who would even know that I Existed, but The Lord Kept me in His Hands, The Lord Hid me from many things that a normal person has liberty to achieve for the main purpose of His Will and Glory Being Established. I say again, to God Be All The Glory, Great things He Has Done.

Let us seek to look into The Words of God, then I will explain that which The Lord Has Shown to me to write.

St Matthew Chapter 28:16-20.

"Then the eleven disciples went away into Galilee, into a mountain where Jesus had appointed them. And when they saw Him, they worshipped Him: but some doubted. And Jesus came and Spake unto them, Saying, All Power is given unto Me in Heaven and in Earth. Go ye therefore, and teach all nations, baptizing them in the Name of The Father, and of The Son, and of The Holy Ghost: Teaching them to observe

all things whatsoever I have Commanded you: and, lo, I Am with you always, even unto the end of the world. Amen".

1 John Chapter 5:4-7.

"For whatsoever is born of God overcometh the world, and this is the victory that overcometh the world, even our faith. Who is he that overcometh the world, but he that believeth that Jesus is the Son of God?

This is he that came by water and blood, even Jesus Christ; not by water only, but by water and blood. And it is The Spirit that beareth witness, because The Spirit is Truth. For there are three that bear record in Heaven, The Father, The Word, and The Holy Ghost: and these three are one".

Now let's look into that which God Is Revealing through this Topic called The Authority: The Lord Reveals that there is only One Authority which is God, but within The Authority of God there are difference in measurement that it is seen that one level of God's Authority can never be compared to another level of God's Authority and in the same breath all the Levels of God's Authority is still equal to the full Volume of that which is God's Authority.

This demonstration seeks to explain to us as Children of God that we can only be exposed to the level of Authority that we have found ourselves to climb, and that responsibility solely depends on the Child of God that is climbing in God. A Child of God can only know God to the level that they must know God based on their Spiritual Hunger of desiring to feed in God as much as they can.

The Lord Reveals that The Authority of Father Is Holy, Unlimited, Eternal, Complete Power, Almighty, Light in its Fullest Measurement, Complete Spirit, Full Glory and absolutely No Weakness, No Beginning, No Ending, No Aging, Lives Forever, does not Look Up because there's NOTHING Above Father. Now because of this Full Measurement of Father the only thing that is deemed worthy to be in the surroundings of Father is The Holy Celestial beings that can stand to be in The Presence of Father without being totally consumed by The Full Nature of Father.

The Lord Reveals that The Authority of Son which is Jesus Christ is the Only Spiritual Bridge from Father to mankind thus granting mankind access to approach Father through the Sacrifice of Jesus Christ. Jesus Christ Is Father but to a lower Manifestation and Authority of what the Full Nature of Father Truly Is. Now by having access through Jesus Christ, a Child of God will always have the pathway to touch Full Authority without the consequences of touching Full Authority which is death, because Jesus Christ Is Always Linked to The Full Authority of Father and yet still remains the One and Only link for the Physical.

The Lord Reveals that The Authority of The Holy Ghost is to put all other spirits under subjection of that which Father Requires in His Will Being Done. The Holy Ghost Cannot be defeated because God is not defeated. If the vessel in which The Holy Ghost was dwelling is defeated, it simply means that such a person's vessel is corrupted or damaged based on the disobedience of that person towards The Direct Will of The Holy Ghost. Therefore the soul and temple of that person is defeated and not The Holy Ghost which cometh from God and is of God.

This statement will suggest to my Readers that we can indeed lose The Gift of The Holy Ghost. It was Given by Father and it can be Taken away by Father. Jesus Christ when He was about to die cried Father, why hast thou forsaken me because He Felt The Holy Ghost Departing the Temple. The Holy Ghost is The Full Nature of God in portions thus The Holy Ghost Still Maintains The Full Characteristics of God which is Holiness, thus that which is Holy cannot suffer the presence of corruption. Jesus Christ was about to experience corruption through death thus The Holy Ghost Had to

Move because The Holy Ghost cannot suffer to see corruption. If our Temple disobeys the guidance of The Holy Ghost, then The Holy Ghost will not remain within our vessel because the vessel will now become corrupted.

The Lord Reveals That Access to Father which is The Full Authority is A Spiritual Ladder, the First step on this Spiritual Ladder is The Holy Ghost which is Clean Spirit, the Second Step on this Spiritual Ladder is Jesus Christ The Son, Mediator, and the Third and Final Access on this Spiritual ladder is The Father which is Full Unlimited Power, and all three manifestation of The Levels of Authority is equal to ONE.

One Authority, One God, One Name, One Church, One People, One Doctrine, One Heaven but difference in Glory; Different Manifestation because there are differences in the glory of who God Is to whosoever is climbing on this Spiritual Ladder to know God for themselves.

Another major fact that The Lord Reveals in this Message is the use of The Name Jesus Christ. Now it is seen, heard and spoken a lot from many Christians that seek to use The Authority of God by limiting what they should actually receive from God.

What do I mean?

It is seen that many that are using The Authority of God have only stopped half way on The Spiritual Ladder. I've heard many Christians praying and ending their Prayers by saying in Jesus's Name! It would suggest that I should automatically know what that means or even better, when we pray like that, God will Automatically know what that means! I wonder If the demons that are fixed to destroy our lives know what it means when we end our prayers by conveniently saying in Jesus's Name?_____.

I've often asked myself why? The last time I checked, no one can use a physical key that was half made to open a door that is shut! It requires the perfect key that is made for that locked door for that person to gain ACCESS! The Authority of God is not in Jesus's Name but rather The Authority of God must be firmly confirmed in The Name of Jesus Christ. And I'll tell you why.

The Lord Reveals to me that The Name Jesus by itself speaks to The Authority that is only on the Earth, that which is already manifested and replicated of which many have seen a type of deliverance like that before. Jesus, this is the Humanity / Vessel of the Sacrifice that was offered for Man's fall from The Spiritual. The Lord Reveals to me that when A Child of God uses The Full Authority of The Name of Jesus Christ this confirms with The Authority which is on Earth that is limited to now have full access with The Authority which is in Heaven that has No Limits, which means that through Access of The Full Authority there will always be New Deliverance to experience that was never seen before because of The Connection to Father.

St Matthew Chapter 16:18&19.

"And I say unto thee, that thou art Peter, and upon this ROCK I Will Build My Church; and the gates of hell shall not prevail against it. And I will give unto thee the keys of The Kingdom of Heaven: and whatsoever thou shalt bind on Earth shall be bound in Heaven; and whatsoever thou shalt loose on Earth shall be loosed in Heaven".

Let's give a Revelation on this: The Sacrifice for Man's Fall from Spirituality, The Name is more confirmed to be CHRIST rather than JESUS, but both cannot be separated from the other because together it forms the Unity of The Perfect Sacrifice. Jesus is the Earthly Name or Access or Key to reflect the participation of Adam's Fall for the Sacrifice; and Christ is The Heavenly Name or Access or Key to manifest The Guidance of The Mind of God to link Heaven and Earth in full agreement of ONE AUTHORITY back to The Will of God Being Done.

The Name Christ Speaks towards The Spiritual side / The Mind of God for the manifestation of the same Sacrifice towards The Will of God. The Sacrifice for Man's Fall from Spirituality was not only necessary in The Physical to be confirmed on Earth, but also this same Sacrifice was also fulfilled in The Spiritual First. Therefore The Name which brings forth The Full Authority of The Father cannot and should not be separated because it is not separated, It is One.

- I wonder, when we pray as Children of God, is the requirement from us from our Father positioned at half deliverance?_____.

- Was the death of Jesus Christ made in vain to give us Full Access to The Father?_____.

- Having now Access to Full Authority, why are we only satisfied with half the glass full, when God Requires from us that the glass be always Full to complete our Sacrifice? _____.

I hope this Message has helped at least one person for The Glory of God's Kingdom. If you have received a copy of this Message, do your part and seek to help at least one Soul to make it into God's Kingdom, together we can make a difference in this broken World. I know it is seen that these Messages are now being presented in book format, now I've made it very clear to those who cannot afford to buy the Books that if you're able to contact me, I will send some of the Messages to you according to that which you find yourself experiencing in this life.

To The God of Excellent Intelligence be all Glory, Honor and Praise. Thank you Father for Using me for Your Glory, in The Name of

Jesus Christ I Pray. From Pastor Lerone Dinnall and The Ministry of The Church of Jesus Christ Fellowship, Savannah Cross, Jamaica, West Indies. God Bless.

Use The Authority, Don't Dilute The Authority!

SOMETHING IS WRONG WITH THE INPUT...

Message # 162   **Date Started October 28, 2020**
Date Finalized October 28, 2020.

Wise words coming from The Late Bishop Austin Whitfield, still teaching even though he's gone to rest:

"Words that come with the intention to change my focus just pass from one ear to the next, I do not allow those words to be planted within my Soul"!

Greetings family of God in The All Powerful Name of Jesus Christ, The Name that is able to break chains and to set the captives free, The Name that is so Powerful that many who desire to pray can never use The Full Measurement of The Name Jesus Christ but stops at jesus's name or declare in the name of jesus.

I wonder for a long time what does it actually means when someone or a ministry seeks to minister to people's lives about The King of kings and then to conclude that which they are saying in jesus's name or in the name of jesus, I'm confused because I never find it difficult to use The Full Name of Jesus Christ being a Minister of Religion, even when I pray personally for myself and family for the Church family, I need God's Full Attention, therefore, I cannot afford to find myself being halfway on The Spiritual Ladder or Nowhere on The Spiritual Ladder.

Now what is mostly disturbing about someone, a minister, a ministry praying and doing what they are doing and conveniently ending by saying in jesus's name or in the name of jesus is that for me the person listening to that prayer, Spiritually, that term jesus's name or in the name of jesus can mean so many different things and have so many different directions has to where that prayer is going and to who that prayer is really being offered to. I don't know about my readers but I personally cannot afford to pray not even for one second and that prayer is not being channeled to The True Source of Deliverance, not even for a second; I have to make certain that my prayer is as straight as an arrow leading in the direction that it must be going.

Learn this: The devil is no fool, in order to confuse the truth he has to manipulate the very truth, check for yourself in the beginning of time even in Eternity, there is always a manipulation of the truth by the seed and the spirit of the devil. When someone says in jesus's name or in the name of jesus, what does it mean? _____.
What should it mean for a person that is serving The True and Living God? _____.
Does it mean that such a person is directly offering their prayers in The Name of Jesus Christ? _____.
Let's think about this for a minute, can it mean that a person can disguisedly pray to a deity or idol under pretense to mislead those who are listening to that prayer?_____.

What if at the end of such prayers that are made in jesus's name or in the name of jesus the true meaning is saying and being directed in the name of jesus baal, or in the name of jesus lucifer or in the name of jesus lodge practices or in the name of jesus obeah and witchcraft practices, what if?_____.
At least if I say In The Name of Jesus Christ, that's final, everyone understands what I'm saying including Heaven.

I know what many are going to say, that I'm being too technical but through everything in Life, Health, Wealth, Family and Religion, Which of these is a must to make certain that it is completely 100%

Pinpoint accurate to The Source? _____.
If our Religion is not on The Foundation to manifest in our lives then how are we ever going to be able to establish Pure Health, Strong Wealth and a Solid Family, How, and When, if Ever?_____
_____.

It is so convenient for someone to just say in jesus's name or in the name of jesus that we never stop to think about what they are really saying and who they are really praying to. It would seem like it is so exhausting to mention The Full Authority of The Name of Jesus Christ that whenever we are now praying it's best to just shorten The Name by saying in jesus's name or in the name of jesus. I wonder if I'm the only person that has a problem with this type of prayer, If I don't find any problem with declaring and decreeing The Name of Jesus Christ why should any other Minister of Religion find a problem with Declaring The True Undiluted, Undisputed, Anointing Filled, Approval Filled, Access Approved, Demon Chasing Name of Jesus Christ from their lips, WHY, WHY, WHY?_____.

My Apology to those who pray in this manner and they know that their prayers are being channeled through The Access Name of Jesus Christ. But that's the main Problem, we just don't know who is genuine from those who are fake because everyone has suddenly picked up the doctrine in prayer by declaring and decreeing in jesus's name ...., or in the name of jesus......., True Child of God should worry about this practice, how do you now screen when everyone has the same spirit or spirits of the cushion of jesus's name and in the name of jesus.

My Question is still WHY? _____
_____.

I think that's a question that will never be answered, it will suddenly be rectified little by little I hope because some people are reading The Bible and it's like worst that Chistopher Columbus Discovering a new Island, they've never seen The

Name Christ and worst they don't know The Revelation of The Name CHRIST, that disturbing being a Minister of Religion or a Ministry, who and where are people being directed to? _____.

I'm just here to do my part of The Ministry of Jesus Christ, someone else will always continue The Ministry of Jesus Christ because God Is Never Short of Vessels to Use. This wasn't my main focus but when The Spirit of God Flows to write in a direction, who can question that which God Has Declared?_____.
When it is certain that we have a new generation that is ready to take charge of their responsibilities that are being trained in the wrong path, this should raise some concerns not only for the Ministry but for life.

Remember that all was well with The Children of Israel as long as there was still someone to train the upcoming generation in the right path but as soon as training was stopped concerning Who their God Was, that's where the real problem came in, if we don't know we can never walk in a pathway that was not made knowledgeable, therefore we can never train ourselves to make certain that we train our children therefore we will be placed in bondages based on that which we were initially trained to fulfill from those who are our teachers for today.

It's easy to learn how to Pray the wrong way, it's called ignorance, we just do what everyone else is doing without identifying the path that leads to The Source, how to pray to our Father must be a **MUST KNOW** so that we can past on the knowledge to our children to follow in our footsteps. Something Is Wrong With The Input... It's clear understanding to know that whatever comes in the vessel is the same that brings its manifestation from the same vessel.

There are some people A Child of God must never seek to cause those people to remain within your circle because people will build you Spiritually and also the wrong set of people will break you Spiritually.

There are some people that has is their mission's menu for our lives to keep us limited, they cannot afford to allow us to think and manifest in a standard that will replicate Spiritual Growth and at the same time there are those Special individuals that God Has placed in our lives that are like Spiritual Building Blocks, even if you don't want to do something because you have not seen yourself in that position as yet, Special people with unbiased Spiritual Strength will Push and Force us to do extraordinary things that are amazing to realize before our very eyes.

There are some people that will instead use us as stepping stones to progress themselves to where they think they can reach as long as where they have now reached, to themselves it's somewhere that they can always look down on us to say that's where we should remain. Remaining under the influence of such persons is Spiritually damaging because if influence is not broken that means that influence is still in effect for that vessel. Change is something that only the man in the mirror can effect, no matter how hard and long someone prays for a person for change that person will never change if they do not see for themselves that they are the person that needs to start moving in a direction of change from that which held them in bondage to that which is going to Spiritually lift them out of Spiritual Prison instituted by people, but change must start from within.

There are some people that cause you to keep counting pennies because everytime you see them their only conversation to you being their best friend is about pennies but for themselves to elevate their standings in life their conversation is never about pennies but rather expressing the need of earning thousands of dollars so that they can keep the feed of penney conversations to those who is under their control. There are those Special People that God Has Hand Picked for our journey of life that every time they reach for themselves another step into prosperity they are immediately encouraging their friend with the same process of knowing how to also make a further step into prosperity and growth. There are some people that will hide from their friends the pathway of success because that way is just too good for you but Special People will always reveal every path of success for their friend to also walk through.

It's Good to speak about Special friends but there is one True Friend that Never Disappoints, His Name Is Jesus Christ, not jesus but Jesus Christ, jesus is an imposter, a bastard child because the name jesus does not have his father's name, it's always a wonder as to what is jesus's name. Jesus Christ Representation is found in all the Special people that God Has placed within our lives that Builds us, that Inspires us, that Tells us to never give up when there is no physical reasons for us to hold on, Jesus Christ Tells us about Gold and never about pennies, these Special People that Represents Jesus Christ they will Push and Pull us to continually being a better version of ourselves and always pray for us to climb Spiritual Steps to reach The Continual Higher Level in God.

On the other hand is jesus ...., whatever his last name is ...., jesus........., this term represents those people that are only around to spy and discover our next move on the path to Spiritual Growth to put stumbling blocks of discouragement, to always take away that which we do have and is never in a position to give to advance that which we are, jesus........., whatever his last name is will always distract us from positive things, he'll sit on us and tell us it is for our good just as long as we remain committed to be his eternal friend; jesus ...., oh, wait a bit, I still don't know your last name........., he will continuously offer empty promises and even make us believe that what belongs to God for His Glory can be in the possession of a servant.

We can never trust jesus........., because he refuses to tell us his last name and through teachings we know that the last name is where the inheritance is fixed, jesus......... is always being made known partly but at the same time is also hiding fully. A man and a woman meeting each other for the first time, if the last name is not known then only a foolish person would continue the conversation, jesus   , sounds like a deciever to me, why do you just say the name jesus.........., but have not presented to me the true name that I can search the lineage of your descendance, jesus.........., just that! Ok, it's jesus's name.........., No thank you, I still need more than that! Never in history has someone that was born been called by only one name, jesus.........., not even a middle name!

The suspense is killing me because I've learnt that before I accept I must know the full volume of what I'm Accepting. So tell me the last name of this jesus.........., I need to see if it's the same Jesus Which Is The Christ, The Son of The Living God, The God That Was, That Is and That Is To Come, The Almighty God. If there is someone that knows this jesus.........., could you please let me know his last name so that I can compare and see if it's The Same Last Name of My Lord and Saviour Jesus Christ. The Name of Jesus Christ, it's just so easy to say, Wow, Look at that, almost no effort to just say Jesus Christ or Jesus The Christ.

It becomes so ridiculous when someone bypass The Easy Access Name of Jesus Christ to just merely say in jesus's name.........., has anyone noticed that this jesus cannot give his last name.........., still waiting for the name that is a mystery that so many Preachers and Teachers, Bible Scholars and Radio Announcers and Television Ministers and Ministries have been repeating day in, day out, night and day, jesus.........., jesus ...., jesus ...., What Is The Name?_____.
Please give me the name that I can joint with you in Divine Holy Prayer but without The Name I can't be in agreement with that which I still don't know your savior's name, and don't say the name is jesus only because that name is short, and don't say in jesus's name because I don't know what is beyond that name.

It's so easy to say Jesus Christ, it makes you wonder why so many make it look so difficult to say; Oh, I know! I get it; whenever The Full Access of The Name Jesus Christ is repeated it invokes The Source of All Authority and many times those that have an hidden purpose truly don't want to get The True and Living God Involved, because if God Is Called and the altar is not clean or the sacrifice was not being presented and made ready to The Clean God then those who have called on The Name of The Clean God Jesus Christ knows that their altar will not stand if Clean just have a Look on that which is dirty, so I understand; go ahead, call on the never known gods of jesus.........., As for myself and my house and Ministry, The Saving Name Of Our God Is JESUS CHRIST, THE ALL KNOWING, ALL MIGHTY GOD.

Truth, we are currently living in a world that jesus ...., is so much more popular that JESUS CHRIST, I kid you not, examine for yourself and listen to understand Spiritually, on the radio programs, television programs, internet, place of worship, the unknown or the known jesus........., is mostly praised, glorified and given honor for most of what he is not deserving of, check for yourself because most Christians are ignorant, over 80% of prayers, declarations, dedications and ministry's effort are concluded in the name of jesus ......, or jesus's name........., whether it's being offered to Jesus The Christ no one really knows because the mediator of these prayers and dedications leaves everyone in limbo by saying in jesus's name........., or in the name of jesus ......, 20% of mediators end their conclusions in The Name of Jesus Christ or in The Name of Jesus Christ of Nazareth, Truth! How strong is our God manifest also the surety of how much we know our God.

It's always the Input a Child of God needs to be concerned about, feed yourself with the right information, surround yourself with the right people, identify The True and Living God and never the gods that only copy off the original Character of The True and Living God. The name jesus is being copied because of its earthly manifestation but The Sovereignty of Jesus Christ can never be copied or replicated thus those who know The Name Jesus Christ know The True Authority that is in The Name.

Blessings people of God in The Only Access Name of Jesus Christ, to God Be All Glory, Honor and Praise through The Only Access

Name of Jesus Christ. I hope that this message will become a guide-line for those who have accepted The Truth. From Pastor Lerone Dinnall and The Ministry of The Church of Jesus Christ Fellowship Savannah Cross, Jamaica, West Indies. God's Blessing Continually.

Jesus Christ Inputs Manifest Heaven's Reward, jesus......., whatever his name is will manifest that spirits are now invited in the vessel to Steal, Kill and to Destroy. Truth!

STOP INVESTING IN OIL AND BEGIN INVESTING IN ANOINTING FROM GOD!

Message # 136   Date Started June 16, 2020.
                                 Date Finalized June 16, 2020.

1 Samuel Chapter 16:14-18.

"But The Spirit of The Lord Departed from Saul, and an evil spirit from The Lord Troubled him. And Saul's servants said unto him, Behold now, an evil spirit from God Troubleth thee. Let our lord now command thy servants, which are before thee, to seek out a man, who is a cunning player on an harp: and it shall come to pass, when the evil spirit from God is upon thee, that he shall play with his hand, and thou shalt be well. And Saul said unto his servants, Provide me now a man that can play well, and bring him unto me. Then answered one of the servants, and said, Behold, I have seen a son of Jesse the Bethlehemite, that is cunning in playing, and a mighty valiant man, and a man of war and prudent in matters, and a comely person, and The Lord is with him".

Let Us Pray...

Father of Heaven and Earth I Come before Your Presence only through The Access Name of Jesus Christ. Father, I am Your Son, and I seek to remain as a child in Your Hands for Your Eternal Spirit to Continually Guide my steps, that whatever has been written by my hands to bring forth Divine Revelations of spiritual wickedness in high places and the operations of evil altars, that whatever is written by me it will remain to be that which The Almighty God Has Revealed, therefore, I didn't say what these Messages Revealed by my own thoughts, because my words are vanity and means nothing without Your Spirit, nor can it bring forth any fruits for future manifestation, but Father, when You Speak, The Heavens are Moved out of its place, the Earth must Shake, The Confirmation must be Identified in Heaven and also upon Earth that The God of The Entire Universe have just Spoken what is His Will Being Done. Father, I remind You that I'm just a Vessel in Your Hands, it's never my will, it's rather always Your Will Being Fulfilled. In The Name of Jesus Christ Receive All Glory, Honor and Praise, Amen.

Greetings Family of God in The Matchless Name of Jesus Christ. It's a joy to again be writing for The benefit of The Kingdom of God. Wow! Here we go again. When I got this Topic from The Lord I hesitated for about two days, because I'm well aware of what this topic is going to reveal, because it's something that crossed my pathway on numerous occasions with negative effects of it's manifestation, therefore I'm Knowledgeable of The Divine Power that this Message will Reveal and also The Strength that it will Release for those who are serving God with Clean Hands and a Pure Heart.

The Topic Says: Stop Investing In Oil And Start To Invest In Anointing! What am I Saying: What Is The Spirit of God Saying To His People? _____.

There are many of God's People that have been fooled to identify The Manifestation of The Movement of God within a vessel because we've not yet understood that the devil is no fool, but rather, the devil is smart, ph.D graduate with honors. There is something that I have learnt in Church growing up in Sunday School by The Late Bishop Austin Whitfield, and he always taught The Church that whenever we are going on an Interview or something that is important to channel the future of our development, he would always teach us that we should always put our best foot forward because first impression always last. This is saying that whoever we're being interviewed by, they are alway fixed within that one interview or that one delivery of who we say we are to be true and it is the full outcome of our lives based on that one interview or opportunity.

The Lesson from The Great Man of God was and is of great value, however growing in The Spirit of God will always branch New Education in the walk of this life. The Spirit of God Teaches The Comfort of The Holy Ghost, therefore letting the person that is being taught knows what it feels like when The Presence of God is with that person, and it's a common understanding to also identify when it is that The Presence of God is not with that person. What I'm Identifying to my Readers is that even though your a person that have Received of The Holy Ghost and feels The Full Fellowship of The Holy Ghost, there are times that will and must present itself that it is felt by that same person who is in fellowship with God to now feel the atmosphere of Spiritual Loneliness. This manifestation can be caused by different factors.

1. **This person that was once in Fellowship with God and has now found themselves out of Fellowship with God can be the result of sin. The moment A Child of God sin, The Presence of God Must Move. When A Child of God now becomes again clean for God's Use, The Presence of God Will Return, unless it was a sin that was committed from this person that marks in The Spiritual as being a Sin Against God. Now if this happens that means that**

True Fellowship that was experienced with that person from God will be no more received for entertainment.

2. This person that was once in Fellowship with God and now finds themselves in a Spiritual lonely environment from The Fellowship of God and have not sinned as far as they know for themselves. This Child of God maybe experiencing Spiritual Growth from God, of which everything that you've previously learnt, God is now Calling that servant to A Higher level to Unlearn certain things that they have learnt, because some of the things which we have learnt in this life, it's dominance is coming from the prince of this world, therefore, that which we have learnt will act as a Spiritual prison for us thus putting Spiritual shackles on our feet preventing us from Spiritual Growth. Spiritual Growth is a Must in Fellowship with God, but spirits of different training are never welcomed in the process of Spiritual Growth In God. In this time of Growth process, God Will Identify to that Child of God exactly what it is that is affecting the need of Spiritual Growth for that Child of God to again feel The Comfort of The Presence of God with them.

3. This Child of God that was once in Fellowship with God and remains in Fellowship with God, that feels The Separation of God's Presence from their walk or from their talk or from an activity or from an interview or opportunity for life's success. I've always said this to The Church:

"God Is Not Stupid; We Are At Times Stupid,
    That's Why We Fall Into Traps"!

The Clean Presence of God Will Not, Cannot, Can Never Come In The atmosphere and presence of that which does not move in agreement with God's Will Being Done. Therefore A Child of God that knows that they are Growing in God, but for some strange reason you went for what you think is a great opportunity to advance the development and future of your life, in that occasion it was now learnt by that Child of God an important lesson that only God can Teach, to see for yourself that The Presence of God that is within you is not pulling and pushing you in that moment of time to be apart of what you think and what the world has taught you to believe is a wonderful opportunity that you must seek to impress to thus receive that opportunity. The Spirit of God which Entertains The Presence of God is always Seeking for Continuation for the vessel it is being Entertained by, thus The Spirit of God which is now binding to our own abilities to make us look splendid and great in whatever it now desires for us to be great in, this same Spirit of God will Allow for us to look stupid, lack of greatness, undesireable to anyone that sees us, just to hide that Child of God from that which we think is of great value for our lives, but have not yet understood that we have not yet attained The Level of Anointing that will cause for us to Transform that same opportunity with that same atmosphere to be in Obedience of The True Spirit of God that Rules our lives. Because of Continuation from The Spirit of God which Entertains The Presence of God, that opportunity is spoiled for the moment so that the spirits that truly have governance of that atmosphere will not corrupt the vessel for the Use of God's Spirit Continuation.

I grew up in Church, not attending Church but rather had the opportunity to Grow Up In Church, I needed my Readers to understand the difference. There is probably not a message or a sermon that I have not heard about or heard something like that before, this was strictly implemented by The Late Bishop Austin Whitfield.

"My House, My Rules"!

Bishop Whitfield made certain that everyone within the rule or covering of his house had to attend Church, whether you like it or don't like it, you have to go or find somewhere else to live. He would say these words:

"Either You D-O or You G-O"!

I learnt about prayer meetings that it was always best to start praying to God before the Sun begins to pray to God, this was observed by Bishop Whitfield. I learnt about Fasting and Fasting services and the discipline in this must be for each Child of God to seek for Perfection In Sacrifice. I learnt about Sunday's Worship, this is the day that Full Discipline for the Sacrifice must be Achieved. Bishop Whitfield never eat food for any Sunday's Service, he went on Fasting because he wanted to be completely Focused for God's Mission for that Day, going to Church with him walking on the road, if someone seeks to have a conversation with Bishop Whitfield on Worship days, they would not be entertained, that's how Focused he was. You would always hear him say:

"Later, When Service Is Finished I'll Talk With You".

I learnt A lot from Bishop Austin Whitfield, I learnt a lot from Church and am still learning a lot from Church, it's a never ending class room. I learnt a lot from Manifestations in Church, to identify Good Manifestation and also Bad Manifestation. I always realized that when some people came to Church just to put on a show, how Bishop would react based on that person's manifestation, and I also observed how Bishop Whitfield would react around people and Saints that had The True Manifestation upon their lives, and the response was completely different because of the difference in manifestation. I've observed that people from the past was fixed being obsessed with The Blessing that God Would Release whenever there was a True Sacrifice Given to God, that same behavior is also seen in the present day, the Cain and Abel manifestation, they are dead for a long time now but the spirits still exists, this prove to us as Children of God that we are never fighting with the person that we see next to us, it's rather spirits.

Now because of this continuous unclean spirit or spirits that is still living and will live until The Kingdom of God is finally come, A Child of God has to be continually Focus of the threats of spirits manifestation in vessels, and what these spirits will do at any cost to remain being fed through the activities of these vessels lead by spirits.

I've learnt from Church and life that a person with spirits will use different abominable things and go through different abominable practices to gain more spirits so that the foundation spirit can remain being fed. Everyone is born and granted special gifts or talents from God The Father, but there are those that have received the foundation spirit of Iniquity that are not satisfied with the gifts and talent that God Has Given and seeks for more, not from God that Gives to all man freely if we ask, there are those that comes in contact with Special and Gifted individuals that remain Clean to God that have acquired something of purpose from that individual and use it to spiritually pull from that individual what is their God Given Talent Released by God. And if A Child of God is Stupid it will also happen to you. There are some things that being Children of God must not be given any access to anyone that is not in your immediate Circle, and even some of the times our Circle is filled with the devil's children and we don't even know.

Fact: We are not all God's Children. There are more of the devil's children in this life than those who are God's Children, remember that!

There is this Phrase that is called the Oil, or have Oiled that is mentioned by those who considers themselves to be untouchable because of their OIL. Note, I never said The Anointing or The Anointing Oil, I said the Oil. Now let's explain what is meant when you hear someone mention a term called the Oil or their Oil or they have rubbed in their Oil. I came across this term when someone stole some bathroom fixtures from The Church, and the person was well known even to Police, but there was this term mentioned that confused and frustrated my Spirit that was spoken by Individuals that this man uses his Oil, and no one can catch him because he uses his Oil.

And this is the Main Problem that The Eternal Father has with us: **"The Difference"**! Anything that is different from that which a person truly is, is directly linked to that which is called the other gods, because they have used different spirits to bring to manifestation that which they are manifesting.

Let's give an example: Let's say we have Brother A that has Seven talents from God, and let's say we have Brother B that have only received one or two talent from God, now nothing is wrong with both these two brothers why God Gave them Different Gifts, because at all times God Will Release to the Vessel that which the vessel has in potential to fulfill for His Glory. There is a war in The Spiritual That has been in manifestation before time came into existence, and that War is for spirits to continually seek to rise to the Position of where Spirit Is. If Brother A and B were able to appreciate that which God Has Released for their vessels to have to thus fulfill, it would be excellent, but that's not the case. If Brother A or B entertains the spirit of Iniquity then that spirit of Iniquity must birth the spirit of Envy and when envy has received its full course of feeding in that vessel, it will bring forth a spirit with the name of that baby is called Greed, and greed says it all:

"I Want To Feed, I Must Feed, Whatever I Must Do To Feed I Have To Do It No Matter The Consequences"!

Now at this time of Greed spirit's feeding, it will be realized that whoever that has a talent or gift from God, if this person with the spirits have come in contact with anything that is of value to a person with gifts and great abilities from God, then that item which is of value to the person that remains clean from spirits will grant Access to that person's abilities and gifts from God when it is that the person that is entertaining spirits have espoused that item of value to a demon whose practice is in False altars, Diviners, Lodge, Necromancers, Witches, Obeah Man or Woman, Principalities and Powers, Dark Forces of the devil etc.

That one item of value from someone that is Clean and True also has in it the Clean and True Virtue from that person, and with this clean and true virtue anyone of the dark world can spiritually pull The True Anointing from that person to anywhere in the world, that person no longer have to be in the same room as the other person to now become Oiled with The Abilities and Gifts from God that was original Placed on the person that God Has Anointed. The person with spirits now becomes Oiled by spirits with great abilities and gifts.

There is one thing to know, The Anointing of God Can and Will Break any strong hold upon any Child of God that has experienced the captive of their Anointing to the Dark and evil altars of the enemy, but The Key for this Child of God is to continue to Grow In God, you may have been touched by the devil at one point in your life by means of evil people that you have given access within your Circle, but that's not the end. At the point in your life at the level of which you were in God, yes, that Anointing was touched, but if you can learn through The Spirit of God very quickly how to now flush your Circle and now find yourself putting Heaven's Padlock around The Spiritual Chain that is around your Circle, then A Child of God will automatically put a Spiritual Stop from the Pulling of that Child of God's Anointing by the use of the dark forces of this world. Because at the point in your life that something of value was removed from your Circle to be used by a means to hold you down, if this Child of

God Seeks The Face of God for themselves, then God Will Introduce to that Child of God The Spiritual Ladder that will force Spiritual Growth by the only means of a Now Separation with God.

The level at where you were when your feet was tangled in spiritual traps, because of Spiritual Growth from God along with Firm Separation from things and people of darkness, that Child of God will be more appreciating the mistakes and unfortunates of the past because the past experience is and always will be one of the best Instructors.

Many in the world are even blinded by the use of people that have used Oil of Abominable practices, because the eyes of a man still remains to be the main source for judgment, whatever looks good to the eyes of the physical is accepted by the soul of that person, therefore that Oiled person has past the test of whatever opportunity that is laid out for that person to receive if they have past that test of Physical eye examination.

When A Child of God begins to Grow in God, the physical senses are still there because it paves the pathways to understand The Spiritual Senses that were always there but locked away from that person because there is no Spiritual Growth Key to unlock the Hidden Abilities from God.

A Child of God that continues to Grow in God will immediately identify someone that is anointed by Oil from that of A Child of God that is filled or full with The Anointing from The True Clean Spirit of God. It cannot hide, it may take a while, but there is going to be a change in The Spirit's Flow upon your life whenever that person finds themselves within your surroundings again.

I wonder, what is it that they are now seeking within your surroundings or Circle at this time, seeing that when you have Grown and continue to Grow in God, those with spirits of abominable practices cannot remain around your Circle because the spirits is going to become uncomfortable because of the difference in Glory that now exists around your Circle. You, the individual that has Grown in God will also Observe the difference in The Flow of The Spirit of God that is within your vessel just to identify to you also the difference in the Glory or no glory that is in people.

Now understand, A Child of God has to become Vigilant, Top Focused, Spiritual Eyes seeing everything of the movement and manifestation of spirits, and most important, do not allow anyone that comes within your Circle to take away anything of value from your Circle or else you've just began the process of Spiritual Transfer all over again, and this time we have no one to blame but ourselves, because before we were Naive, A Dunce towards the plans, traps and movement of spirits; now we've been Spiritually Educated by The Master of all spirits, His Name Is Jesus Christ The God of The Universe.

Those who have used the abominable Oil to get where they are must continue to use that Oil to remain where they are and even to advance to greater opportunity in life, thus if they can no longer receive another item of value from someone who is Spiritually Clean, then they are going to find someone else that they can have access to get in their Circle to retrieve something of value from that person so that they can use that item to make more abominable Oil to thus continue to RUB in order for the manifestation of the spirits to pull Anointing from Clean Vessels to allow that person who is using the abominable Oil to remain in the position where they are so that spirits can continue to be fed.

I was speaking to a Sister of The Church who is also an employer for her business, I never knew that what I told her today would be of benefit for this Topic. We were speaking about production in people, and I was letting her know that The Lord Reveals to me that there are two types of people in this world, one set of people will Add to your Circle benefits and blessings and will later cause your Circle to begin Multiplying in that same benefits and blessings; the other set of people will cause for your Circle to enter into a trench of disappointments, hardship and struggles, that it will be identified that these set of people came with the spirits to Subtract from your Circle and if they remain within your Circle they will now cause for your Circle to go in a state of rapid Division, thus one day you will end up with a Circle that is completely empty of its resources and benefit from The Father Above. The value of this talk was to make this sister know the type of people that should be allowed to remain in a person's immediate Circle.

Another thing The Lord Has Revealed is that A Child of God that is Growing Spiritually must make certain that whoever comes within their Circle they must trace that person's every steps while they are within your Circle, and even if that Child of God cannot Physically be in every position where that person moves within your Circle, that Child of God must appoint persons who are most trusted within their Circle to watch every steps and movement of people with spirits within your Circle, because not only can someone with spirits **TAKE** something from your Circle to cause harm to your Circle, but that person can also **LEAVE** something within your Circle that will bring forth the same effects of Spiritual Transfer. There is a difference though, if they Take something from your Circle, you may not even remember that item, but if they Leave something within your Circle, The Manifestation of The Spirit and Presence of God **MUST REVEAL A DIFFERENCE WITHIN YOUR CIRCLE UNTIL YOU HAVE FOUND WHAT WAS LEFT BY spirits.**

For those who use the abominable Oil, even if they succeed for a good while, there is always a day of reckoning, it will one day be revealed, and God's People that are Growing in God cannot be fooled, because we Know The Difference from abominable Oil from that of Anointing from God. It is even seen in many work environments those that have been Oiled for a position but not Anointed for the Position. When The True and Clean People of God have learnt about the abominable Oil and have closed all doors from their Circle to those who are entertaining spirits, when the abominable Oil runs out, then it will finally be revealed that the Oil was never stronger than The Anointing, it's just that The Clean People of God Lacked The **GODHEAD** for the devices of the dark and evil world.

There is a lot of Investment taking place in the world currently, The Spiritual Eye will immediately identify that the Investment is not being made in The Anointing of God but rather the investment is being made in the abominable Oil. Every Investment that is made in the Abominable Oil will sink, must sink because there is no foundation of Righteousness that will cause those investments to remain firm to stand all the Storms of life. But those who have Invested wisely in The Anointing from God, these are the same Investment that God Must Breath upon that will see The Investment of a Mustard Seed Starts to Add, then if the seed remains, it will not only Add to The original Investment, but it will now begin to Multiply in Heaven's Language and God Using Heaven's Calculator to bring forth the final figure without physical measurement for those who have made Investment in Anointing From God.

I hope God's People have learnt some valuable lessons for life's journey, it's not going to be easy, it's never easy, stories in The Bible and life's lesson teaches us that any and every good path is never easy; it's rigid and always challenging, therefore we must be in expectation of rough things in life to come, but hard times for A Child of God must always be considered as Spiritual Foundation to be The Spiritual Strength of The beautiful finish Investment that we will become for God's Use.

To The God of Endless Understanding, Knowledge and Wisdom, to Him Who Is Always High Above All Principalities and Power, Dark forces, Evil altars etc. To The God Who Is Always The Light in all darkness be All Credits, Praise and Glory forever and ever, Amen. From The Ministry of The Church of Jesus Christ Fellowship Savannah Cross.

Jamaica, West Indies. God's Blessing Continually from Pastor Lerone Dinnall.

Seek To Make The Right Investment, Power Is Yours To Choose!

THE ACCURSED THINGS...

The Mystery of the Three days, Thirty days and the Three years.

Message # 170 **Date Started November 24, 2021**
Date Finalized November 25, 2021.

To The God of small speech which manifests itself to become the biggest production that will ever be seen or manifested, to The Lord Jesus Christ be All Glory, Honor and Praise, from Spirituality to Physical manifestation then completion in Spirituality, Amen.

It has been eleven months now since the last message was written by myself through the operation of The Living Spirit of God through this Ministry. I hope that all God's People who were privileged to receive at least one of these messages that it would have manifested within your life The Revelation of Heaven's Change.

Here we have a topic that The Lord Gave, not only was the topic given from The Voice of The Lord, but also three specific instructions that The People of God must hear, in order to know what to keep away from to thus establish a continual Spiritual Growth for themselves and their family and circle.

The Topic is The Accursed Things, I got the liberty to do two Sunday School Teachings back to back on November 14, 2021, also November 21, 2021, just to make certain that The People of God received the full understanding of what this topic is asking The People of God to thus become aware of, so that they will be able to not only recognize dark spiritual threats for themselves but to also know exactly what to do if they find themselves in the position of this type of manifestation. The mention of The Accursed Things was mainly spoken about as a warning to The Children of Israel in The Books of Moses and then it continues for the teachings of Joshua, but after those great leaders passed, there was no mention really or continual teachings to The People of God about The Accursed Things which were a constant reminder under the discipline of Moses and Joshua.

A Child of God seeking to read The Bible for themselves would discover that there are many mentions of the term The Accursed Things, but will also discover for themselves that The Bible remains to be a complete mystery, meaning that there are levels and depths within The Bible, that if A Child of God has not found the discipline within relationship with their Father, then this Child of God will be reading The Bible for years without receiving The Divine Revelations which only God Can Give. It will be observed that the term The Accursed Things is mentioned but the declaration of what is The Accursed Things was never declared.

Upon reading about this topic when I was just a Minister, The Lord Revealed this Topic to me for study, and it was then I discovered that if I'm to teach about a topic like this, I needed to make certain that I'm not repeating the term The Accursed Things without truly identifying exactly what I would be telling The People of God About what is The Accursed Things. This desire within myself birth a Spiritual Hunger to seek God's Speech in regards to this topic called The Accursed Things.

The Lord Revealed to me in the Book Ezekiel Chapter 8 & 9, this concerning The place of worship, God's House where people came and offered their sacrifice to The True God. The Lord Identified through these chapters exactly what it would cause for His Eternal Presence to be removed from a place of worship, this was done by the means of people with different practices for The House of God that caused their actions by The View of God to be declared has an

Abomination to The Living Eternal Presence of God that was always at His House, and The Living Presence of God would have Remained at His House if The Discipline of Holiness and Righteousness was maintained to continue. The People of God can read these two chapters for themselves to better understand the displeasure of God in regards to different practices within His Place of worship.

I've personally asked The Lord what is The Accursed Things because The Book Ezekiel demonstrated a lot of things that The Lord will never be pleased with, but the question still remains for a Child of God that is living in this time and age to identify for themselves of what The Bible was referring to when the speech was made about The Accursed Things. The Lord Is Complete in Understanding, Knowledge and Wisdom, which means The GodHead, therefore, The Lord will always Speak to a Child of God at their level with Him for that Child of God to fully understand exactly what question is asked of His Intelligence to Manifest. The Lord Revealed that The Accursed Things Must have the foundation of that which is an Abomination to God, whether it comes in the form of people, places or things, if the identity of anything that is established on the land moves in the direction of that which is contrary to The Movement and Manifestation of The Most High God's Presence, then that same item is the same which will bring forth an Abomination to God, and it is the same that will establish that which is referred to in The Bible as The Accursed Things.

Each Child God can now search for themselves within their own environment to identify anything that speaks to that which is an Abomination to God, then you'll identify for yourselves that which is The Accursed Things. The Lord Gave me Three Instructions about this topic of which I've already taught about it in Sunday School, they are as follows:

Identifying The Accursed Things Manifestations...

1. The Lord Revealed that The Accursed Things has to be Invited within the life, family and circle of A Child of God, this same Accursed Thing **MUST** establish a manifestation around A Child of God's circle within the first Three days, it must be seen and felt because God's Manifestation and Spirit's Flow is completely different and is always repelling against other spirits which are an Accursed Thing. The Lord Revealed that His Spirit's Flow will always grant satisfaction of Abundant Life of whatever level A Child of God is at, therefore, whenever it is seen and felt that A Child of God is no longer satisfy nor can be satisfy with their current abundant life of that which they had no problem with before, this evidence is a manifestation of the invitation of the other gods which births The Accursed Things in the life of this Child of God. Note: The Accursed Things is only a threat to those who are within The Coverage of The Most High God, meaning that this Child of God understands The Flow of The Clean Spirit of God over their lives and knows immediately when The Clean Spirit of God is no longer Flowing over their lives. Remember, within Three days an Accursed Thing Manifestation must be seen by A Child of God and also felt, there must be a difference in your Spirit's Flow from God. The Lord Revealed that this Child of God that has Observed this change within their Spirit's Flow must move quickly to identify exactly what it is that they have Invited within their circle which is an Accursed Thing and seek to remove it quickly.

2. The Lord then Revealed to me that if this Child did not seek to remove that which their invitation allowed being The Accursed Things, and Thirty days have now been expired, then that same Accursed Thing will begin to grow spiritual roots for that Child of God's life, their family and their circle, of which when spiritual roots begin to grow, it will become even more difficult for that A Child of God to now remove that Accursed Thing; in the same breath,

The Manifestation and The Flow of God's Spirit is finding its exist door from that Child of God's life, their family and their circle, because two cannot walk unless they agree, God is in no competition for The Mastery of A Child of God's Vessel. God's Spirit was originally dwelling in that vessel because of Clean Invitation, now that an Unclean Invitation has been granted by the same vessel, God's Spirit can no longer remain in, and around the life of this same Vessel.

3. Third Instruction from The Voice of The Lord to His People, because The Accursed Things was not remove within the first Three days, then it was not rooted out from the life of this Child of God after Thirty days, then it will be the manifestation that this same Accursed Thing will remain for Three years, and after Three years it's only The Action of God through Mercy that can Divinely Remove that which has now become homely within, around and for the complete life of a once Child of God's Circle. Though many prayers and fasting will be made by this Child of God for the restoration of The Clean Spirit of God Flow over their life, this Child of God has to bear the punishment for not removing The Accursed Things within the first Three days, then Thirty days. The wait for removal and restoration of The Clean Spirit of God is Three years, only if God Permits to remove from the spiritual, the root of uncleanness which spells The Accursed Thing, which has now furnished its movement within the life of a once Child of God. The People of God are Warned!

The Accursed Things comes in the manifestation of people, places and things. There are many people that The Spirit of God Demands for us not to get involved with by The Flow of The Spirit of God that Moves inside of our vessels, and we know this to be a fact. There are many things, including money and especially from those who the money is coming from, yes, money is important, it answers and solves problems, but there are some money that are fixed not to bless but rather to destroy the life of A Child of God, and also those money must never find its manifestation within **THE REST** of A Child of God. **REST** meaning, anywhere A Child of God's spirit has the comfort to rest, that being The House of God and also the home of a Child of God. There are people, places and things in the world of which its manifestation is not of God or seeks to acknowledge God, these groups are The Accursed Things that A Child of God must be aware of.

I was making a suggestion to The People of God in Sunday School, that we must become stern towards our place of **REST**, to identify any individuals that would seek to enter our homes to make certain that this same person must be Spiritually Connected to God that they can breathe a word of prayer at the entrance of our gate to thus connect with the manifestation of The Spirit of God within us, that we can confirm within ourselves that whoever is entering our **REST** is the same person that as a direct connection with our Father Above, therefore we are safe or have made the entrance to our life's access a little more difficult to penetrate from The Accursed Things. That's just my advice, Freewill.

I Hope and Pray that this Message was of benefit to The People of God. I hope we have learnt something that we can teach our children so that they can fulfill this walk of life better than us, and with a little more protection of knowing what to stay away from, who to stay far away from and where they must never find themselves.

To The God of Hidden Secrets, Mysteries and Wonders, to Jesus Christ, King of kings and Lord of lords, Amen. From The Ministry of The Church of Jesus Christ Fellowship, Savannah Cross, Jamaica, West Indies. From your Brother, Friend, Minister, and Pastor, Lerone Dinnall. God Bless.

Identify Quickly The Accursed Things...

WATCH THE CHANGE...

Message # 168   **Date Started December 18, 2020**
                             Date Finalized December 18, 2020.

Greetings People of God in The Only Mighty Name of Jesus Christ our Lord and King, Honored to again be in this position of Heaven's Worth to Inspire the lives of God's People in the right direction of Kingdom's Growth. Over the past few days I've been in Divine Lesson with The Father for the main benefit of finding out secrets. The Lord Does this when it is that He Sees that it is now necessary for His Child to gain the knowledge of something which is to come. The Lord Revealed to me that spirit's main weapon is its movements of which I already know because I've learnt it before, but I've found out that when The Lord is Instructing A Child, that Child should never find themselves being in disagreement with that which Their Father is now Instructing. I've learnt this from the Late Bishop Austin Whitfield, and he says and I Quote:

> **"If A Child of God's appearance to God is that they already know something it means that The Lord will never be able to Teach that Child of God anything because the mind is already consumed by what they think they know".**

I've also learnt in School that even if you think you know something, when someone is teaching it is best to be in a mindset to learn even more, even if the material is the same, there is always something new to add to that which you think you know. Therefore, The Lord Revealed at first something that He Already Taught me but that which He Revealed at first was directly linked to that which The Lord would now Reveal next, and this is it: The Lord Revealed that spirit's main weapon is to move just as how it is that Spirit's Characteristic is first to Move, The Lord then Revealed that whenever spirits have been given the approval to attack a Child of God's Circle that Child of God has to identify within the Spiritual and that which they must be mainly concerned about is the type of movements the spirit or spirits will now take form in to activate that which its movement is now sent to consume.

The Lord Revealed to me that the input of anything even though it is disguised at times, this must reveal the output of the same things, thus in order to identify spirit or spirits movement this same Child of God has to understand within The Spiritual the precepts of balancing both Time and Space for their circle. What this means as The Lord would Identify is that many times A Child of God will not be able to filter what is their input which must automatically bring forth that which is A Child of God's output, but if A Child of God can be disciplined to apply The Spiritual to balance both Time and Space of that which is their input then the involvement of Spiritual would have automatically redirect that which was and should be the original output of that which is the first input.

And this A Child of God has to learn very quickly from their Father of how exactly can a servant be granted The Divine Approval to balance both Time and Space for that which a Child of God must calculate. God Is The Ultimate Teacher which means that there is no instruction above His Instructions. The Lord Revealed to me that whenever any input is activated within the lives of His Children, a Child of God MUST first consider the movements of that spirit or spirits, therefore if spirit or spirits is not being fed to activate movements it therefore means that this same Child of God would have found The Spiritual Key of what it means to Balance both Time and Space within The Spiritual to curve or stop that which would have been the fixed outcome of that which is the input.

The Lord Revealed to me that every spirit or spirits movements is fixed to take effect of its movements within the first three days of the original input, three days because spirit or spirit's strength is never Spirit's Strength, thus whatever it is that is the input, spirit or spirits needs the immediate agreement of the vessel it is now injected into to participate in that which the spirit or spirits movements now dictates to be fulfilled.

The Lord Revealed to me that Three Marks The Movements of The Steps Within The Authority of The Father thus the only Spirit that can have full effects after three days without any movement of the original input will automatically reveal that such an input is of Spirit that will dictate the output of Spirit's Input. The Lord Revealed to me that whenever a Child of God receives money that money must be carefully discerned of its spirit or spirits movements because money's energy is fixed with movements, some money has been fixed with the movements to destroy whatever it is now move to whether it be other money, food, clothing, resources, family benefit, once this money is moved with spirit or spirits it must fulfill the destined activity of that which the spirit or spirits is now fueled to fulfill.

The Lord Revealed to me that it is never wise to put money with money, especially those money that you've not identified as its true spiritual source. The Lord Revealed to me that within the time that a Child of God is exercising within The Spiritual that which is known as balancing Time and Space, this same Child of God must always be watchful of the Money's Source to identify manifestation, because if the money is sent and spirit or spirits is not being activated to move to its intended purpose then the source of that money will never be pleased because their money with its spirit's movement to fulfill tasks of destruction will automatically be canceled because spirit or spirit's strength is always limited when Spiritual Balancing of Time and Space is Applied.

The Lord also Revealed to me that it is always best to bring money that is suspicious to Clean Altar because if the money is fixed with unclean spirit or spirits these spirits will never remain for the effects of the money through movements because unclean spirits cannot remain on that which Clean Spirit is now applied to and consecrated on.

To The God of Unsearchable Understanding, Knowledge and Wisdom be All Glory, Honor and Praise from Eternity to Eternity, in The Name of Jesus Christ, Amen. From Pastor Lerone Dinnall and The Ministry of The Church of Jesus Christ Fellowship Savannah Cross, Jamaica, West Indies, God Bless.

Be Disciplined To Watch For The Change...

THE HIDDEN THINGS...

Message # 128

Date Started August 18, 2019
Date Finalized August 23, 2019.

Deuteronomy Chapter 29:29.

"The secret things belong unto The Lord our God: But those things which are revealed belong unto us and to our children forever, that we may do all the words of this law".

All Glory be extended to The Only High God, The Father of The Universe, Jesus Christ The Lamb of God; to The Only God that no one can go above Him, no one can go under Him, no one can go around Him, He Is Supreme In Everything That He Already IS...

I'm rejoicing because of The God that I serve, again this is a great opportunity to be found in this position that I can be God's Chosen Instrument to manifest His Glory and His Will Being Accomplished in the lives of His Chosen People.

A Son of God always has Access to His Father, that's a Fixed Rule that is established within the Spiritual and bears its manifestation in the Physical. There are always things that will take place within the lives of the Sons of God that will now require for that Child of God to now seek His Father who has The Complete Rule and the Decision of all things within His very Hands to Write whatever He Deems fit for a Child of God to face, and this is always done for one purpose, and that purpose is to allow for that Child of God to discover the journey for himself of what it means to find the channel of The Pathway in which The Wave of The Spirit of God is now Moving in.

There are many things that I have written because God Gives me The Approval to write about these things, and His Promise is always:

"No one can touch you in regards to what I Tell you to write".

And again there are things The Lord Has Revealed in Visions that He Told me that this is for your own wisdom to be aware of your own environment, you need not to write about that which I have Revealed for your own Benefit.

Therefore as it stands, there are many secrets that are there, it's not that I don't know, but it is that it should not be revealed until The Father Sees it best that the time has come for that secret to be revealed. And if God Uses someone else to Reveal secrets, it simply means that God Has Equipped that person with The Anointing and The Authority to counteract the effects of those secrets being Revealed. There are many persons in Churches and out of Church that have read what I have written in Messages and in Books, it's not that what I have written is new to them, they know about these things, and they also know what is wrong from what is right, they know what is The True Spirit of God in Operation and they also Know those spirits that are false / fake in operation, but they cannot say anything about it, because they know that they have not been Given The Authority by God to do something about what is being spoken in their ears or what is being manifested in their lives from others. Therefore it is seen that whenever God Begins to Use someone in the capacity to be A Light, even if those who know the Truth does not raise their hands in agreement to that which is Truth, within their Mind, Heart and Soul, The Three Active Response from mankind to God, they would have identified that what is spoken by a Son of God is in Agreement with The Words that Says:

"Let Thy Will Be Done".

Mankind's weakness is SIN, even those of us who are in The Church, Yes, our weakness also is SIN. And because God Has Recognized that we have been Programmed to Sin, God is Always Changing the cards around to always find the Best Available Vessel to Use in which He Can Receive The Full Volume of His Glory from the Vessel that He Is Using. What am I saying? This is what I'm saying: We will never identify in this life that God only has one person to use to manifest His Will and Glory coming forth. That's the main reason why we have Sons of God, there are many Sons of God, and there are many that are being Trained by God to Fill The Position of becoming Sons of God; there are also those who have within their lineage the Promise and The Stamp of God's Approval to become and Remain being Sons of God because of what their parents and their grand-parents preformed for God in His Service, and all these positions of being qualified for the Work of God will still dictate that there is still One God that does the Choosing of who He Deems Fit to Use in the Position that He Require for that Vessel to be used in.

Each Man and Vessel of God Has on them Stamped The Mark Called **PURPOSE**. And once it is identified by God that this Vessel and this person has fulfilled the Purpose that is Destined for that person to fulfilled, then there is nothing that vessel or that person can do about it, because God Has in His Laws Fixed, every man Fulfilling His Purpose if it is that this man will surrender to the Requirements of The Move of The Wave of The Spirit of God.

Even for myself, I know that this talent of writing is a Gift that only God Could Give. Imagine, I never did writing as a subject in School, and in many people's eyes they would never even think that this would be possible for me to do. Before God Called me as a Pastor I never did anything like this, I never even passed English Language in School, and now here I am, God Is Teaching me The Language of The Spirit to know how The Spirit of God Moves in comparison to that of the movements of spirits. Therefore I'm making the best use of this opportunity to write for God's Will Being Done because I Know, as The Lord Have Taught me that the First Manifestation of His Spirit is to MOVE, therefore I know that while The Spirit of God Is Moving over my Life and within My Vessel, I must see to it that I receive all the information that I can

receive from God and be willing to write all the Messages that God Would Allow for me to Write, because when my time is up and my purpose is Fulfilled in writing for God, I know that The Spirit of God will Move to the next Available Vessel that is willing to perform The words that says:

"Let Thy Will Be Done".

I'm somewhat comforted by The Voice of God that Told me that I will be writing a lot more Messages and Books for His Glory. I Say Thank You God for this opportunity to be Used by You. My only Prayer now is that when God would have been finished with me because my time and my purpose is Fulfilled, my Prayer is that The Lord Will Always Remember My Children to consider them also has Available Vessels for His Eternal Spirit to Fill that God Can Use them for His Glory, and also remember my Wife to Use her just the same way The Lord Have Used me, and also The Church, The Altar that The Lord Asked me to Establish, Lord Remember Your Chosen Vineyard to always raise up young men and women that will fight Spiritually for Your Manifested Glory to be done in their lives.

The Lord Revealed to me that every Word that is Released from Him to be Revealed has the effects of Spiritual Authorities, and these Spiritual Authorities are Spiritual policemen that are Released along with The Word of God to ensure that whoever is using The Manifested Word of God are those who have been Anointed and Appointed to do so, or else that person is going to get hurt. It therefore means that a person who is called by God should not try to operate or function in a position that another Child of God is called to operate and function in, because if the shoes doesn't fit, if the Anointing does not match, then the punishment will be Spiritually and Physically unhealthy for all those who seek to Walk, Act, and Operate in a calling that is not their Position or Anointing to do that which is required to be done in that Authority.

"You've Been Warned"!

The Hidden things! I'm going Reveal something to my readers that is going to seem very strange, but anything that concerns God must move directly into The very impossible of Who God Says He Is… I've been experiencing some great challenges regarding the health of my wife, before that it was the health of my children, and that which I've experienced in these situations is the presence and voice of the devil. Now The Lord Has to Grant Approval for a Child of God's Focus and Strength in The Lord to be Tried to thus Establish the Spiritual Environment that which a Child of God can be able to manifest in effectively, this is fixed, as it is our personal process of climbing the ladder of Spiritual Approval.

Now on one occasion that my wife was very sick, fasting never helped, prayer seems like it was going nowhere, it doesn't matter who prayed or who fasted this was something that was fixed just to facilitate the now presence and voice of the devil that spoke these words regarding my wife and my children when they were very sick, and the voice said to me:

"I'm going to kill your wife"! "I'm going to kill your children"!

I heard what the voice said, and I knew that this was not The Voice of God, because this voice and this presence did not bring forth the peace and the approval, the burning and the visions of that which is associated with The Voice of The Living God. This voice rather brought forth a spirit of fear in great measure and also confusions, because at that time you're wondering if you had done something wrong or your wife did something wrong that caused The Presence of God to not have your back in this now difficult time of pain. For about two days I considered what the voice said to me and I realized that in two days that the symptoms of my wife never got worse nor did it get better, but it was as steady as a ship that drops it's anchor in the sea, waiting on my decision of what I believed in, facing the very atmosphere that I am facing. I started to question God about His Promises and asked Him if He was not The God that Told me to Build an Altar for His Glory, I did not get a response; that's how I knew that during any Test that a Child of God is Facing they are always left alone to see for themselves of whose report and whose voice they will now lean on to believe what they must now be born into the Attitude to believe in. I went to the Hospital and laid on the bed of my wife and prayed, and this was my Prayer:

"Lord Jesus Christ, I come before Your Presence this night believing that You are God and that there is no gods before Thee, there is no gods over Thee, there is no gods that can dictate to Thee; Lord, In The Name of Jesus Christ I put the life of my wife in Your Hands, Let Thy Will Be Done, if You See it best to take her life, Let Thy Will Be Done, if it is Your Will to Remove her from my life, then Let Thy Will Be Done, this I pray In The Name of Jesus Christ, Amen".

When I finished my prayer on the bed of my wife in the Hospital, my wife looked at me like she was saying to herself what kind of prayer is that! I kept on repeating: God, Let Thy Will Be Done! I went home and was faced with the same presence and voice of the devil that reminded me of his same words regarding my wife and my children, it was then I realized that I've been receiving these words and these spirits of fear and confusions are accommodating the words that is spoken for over two days now and still nothing happened, I started remembering The Promises of God, I opened my mouth in that Atmosphere of the presence and voice of the devil and said:

"Devil, you said you're going to kill my wife and my children, go ahead; seeing that God Has Given you The Approval to do what you say you're going to do, then go right ahead, do your worse, go and fulfill all that you say you're going to fulfill, because my God Says you can't do nothing that He Did Not Command you to Do, you punk"!

It was then I discovered A New Belief in my God, A Fresh Anointing, A Greater Approval from My Father Above, then I realized that this was what God Needed me to learn, and I had to discover it for myself with no one's help, I had to know that God Is God, and no distractions or confusions or fear or voice from the devil could ever overcome who God Is to His People. The next day my wife was released from the Hospital. Yes, the devil said he was going to kill her, and he got permission from me to go ahead if that is what God commanded him to do. But he could not even walk by her to say hello, much less to take away her life because all God's Chosen People are wrapped up and covered under The Blood of Jesus Christ. Jesus Christ Said:

Revelation Chapter 1:18.

"I Am He that Liveth, and was Dead; and, behold, I Am Alive for evermore, Amen; and have the keys of hell and of death".

This Scripture establishes the fact that no one can live or die unless the permission is Granted by The Only One Man that Died to Repossess The Authority that was once Given to our fore parents being Adam and Eve, and that One Man, His Name Is Jesus Christ. Therefore if we die, we die because it pleases our Father to Grant the Access for us to Die, and we live because our Father Grants The Approval for us to live and have Abundant life through The Blood that Jesus Christ Shed on The Cross for a Perfect Sacrifice.

Therefore devil, you shall be tired to see my face, and not only my face but the face of my wife and my children because that which is wrapped up around our entire life is the word that is called **COVENANT**, and the last time I checked no man living or dead, spirits or demons, not even the devil can cause My God to Break Covenant as long as those who are under Covenant Abide in The Rules of God's Covenant.

I learnt something from this experience, and The Lord would make me understand about the effects of spirits. This is what The Lord Said:

"spirits are 100% what they are, this meaning, whenever A Child of God is being affected by spirits, these spirits never come and affect A Child of God being 50% effective. Therefore every Child of God that is seeking to walk the road of this Christian's Journey has got to find themselves becoming Armored with The Authority that only God Can Give to that Child of God, because when it is the time for the approval to be granted that spirits will now have access to come around our circle, if there is not found in us The Spiritual Fuel to counteract that which these spirits is now enticing us to do, then it is sad to say, but we are going to find ourselves being swallowed by the overbearing effects of that which these spirits now need us to be buried in".

Another thing The Lord Allowed me to understand is that of Spiritual Transfer, I wrote a Message about this already therefore I will not be going into a lot of details about Spiritual

Transfer. The Lord Allowed me to look into what the devil was seeking to fulfill when he told me that he was going to kill my wife and my children, The Lord Allowed me to realize that if I was in agreement and submitted to that which The devil told me that he was going to do, then it would mean that The Authority that God Has Invested within me would have then been transferred to the devil and I will now be left to my new master's will for my life of what he deems fit to take place within my life. But the moment I realized that what the devil was saying was not in agreement with that which

God Had Promised, and I was now able by Free Will to hold on to The Authority and the Promises that God Had Made, it was then that Spiritual Transfer was blocked and the devil realized that he is defeated from trying to plant a seed of Doubt within the life of a Child that is Serving The True and Living God.

The Spirit of Patience is The Key, every Child of God must seek to allow The Gift of Patience to be Born within their lives, we can't be too hasty, whenever it is that voices is speaking to us, we must make certain that we strain the characteristics of each voice to identify the Foundation of each voice Origin. The voice of the devil is always seeking to establish dominion over everything that God Has Established. The Voice of God Will Stand Firm on That which is The Foundation of God's Word.

"You've Been Warned"!

There was also a time when my son got sick and after visiting the doctor three times I was recommended to take him to The Bustamanley Children Hospital, they admitted him in the hospital immediately for meningitis and only one parent could stay with him. I realized that after my son got admitted in the Hospital the next day he was completely fine, no more high fever, the Doctors said that because of the reported illness of meningitis he had to remain in the Hospital for two weeks so that he could receive the full course of treatments that is to be administered, being parents we had to agree with what the Doctors said. But there is a mystery concerning this experience, there are times that God Needs to Step Into the lives of people, but God Cannot Function in our physical environment without a Vessel, if The Spirit of God Functions without A Chosen Vessel it therefore means that we are all DEAD. While praying for my son daily for a speedy recovery even thought there was no more signs of sickness, I then started to ask The Lord what then was the reason for all of this, because everything that happens in life is for a purpose that must be fulfilled whether we have identified that purpose or not, and again we are servants to God, The Journey is never explained to us in full of that which is God's Will Being Done.

I went to visit my wife who was staying with our son at the Hospital, and she confirmed that from the moment he was admitted there was no more sickness that was observed by him, it's like he wasn't even sick. My wife then told me of this parent of which her child is at the same Hospital for four months now, and they have already done three surgeries on the child that was a little over one-year-old, and the surgery that was being done was to correct some internal problems within the child so that the child could eat from her mouth instead of being fed through a straw through the passage of her nose. Therefore, my wife asked me to pray for this Mother that God Would intervene and bring forth a Miracle for her and her child, because at that time the mother was now becoming frustrated because it was being spoken of that the child would die if there was not a successful surgery done for the child.

Before leaving the Hospital that night I took a walk and asked God if He Would Allow for me to pray over this request, I never got an answer. It is important for us being Children of God to Understand The Spiritual Law of Healing, we may have The Gift to perform Healing but The Source Still Remains The Authority of God, therefore no matter what we do, if The Approval is not Granted for us to do what we think we should and must do, then we might find ourselves getting hurt, and now positioning ourselves to draw spirits instead of Declaring and Decreeing that spirits must depart. Yes, spirits can be pulled from vessels and transferred to another available vessel, as well as spirits can be commanded to depart from a vessel and not return to that vessel. All manner of sickness is spirits; we either have The Authority to cast them out or that Authority is not yet Released unto us to do that type of deliverance. And again we have to be careful of those who have Blasphemed God's Authority, they cannot receive deliverance from the spirits that are now plaguing their lives and that of their children, they have Broken God's

Spiritual Law. Again I say that certain things will remain a Secret because Approval is not Granted from God to Reveal Certain Secrets.

I went to my wife and she showed me the mother and the child, we went outside, we talked for a bit, I looked on the child in the hands of her mother and it was one of those moments that everyone knew that if God never did something very soon then that would be it for this child, the child was not looking like an healthy child just having skin and bone, it was then I Felt The Confirmation that I asked God for, that I never received when I prayed at first, this confirmation I will explain in another message because it has to do with The Characteristics of The Spirit of God. When I felt The Approval I asked the mother to put the child in my hands, I looked at the child for about two minutes just to hear what God Was Now Going to Allow me to Decree.

While having the child in my hands The Lord Allowed me to Prophesy to the mother, and this was what God Said to the Mother:

"Thus Saith The Lord, you are now Mine, for years I've Been Calling you to Serve Me and you kept running away from Me, Thus Saith The Lord: I Did this so that you can now surrender to My Will".

The Lord Allowed for me to tell her that He Will Heal her daughter only if she promises that she will now decide to Serve The True and Living God. When The Lord Allowed me to speak those words it was then I discovered the mother crying and acknowledging that this is True and promised that she will now turn over her life in The Hands of God. I looked at the child and the child smiled, The Lord Said Call her Name Destiny, because there will be a great purpose for this child to fulfill. I prayed for the child with The Leading of The Holy Ghost, and The Lord Said this child shall not die because this child is set for His Glory. After praying for that child there were two more mothers that came with their child for prayer before I left that night, two days after the child that was doing the surgery went in again to do another surgery and this time the surgery was a complete success. My experience at the Hospital saw The Lord Allowing me to pray for seven parents with their child and all received A Touch from The Hands of God, to God Be The Glory.

There was also this mother, her name was Kristal, I remembered her name because of someone I knew in the past, I remembered The Lord Specifically Telling this mother that He Will Heal her daughter but the healing process was going to take a little time, therefore when other parents got a word from God that saw an immediate healing and deliverance, of which some of the parents was released before my son was even released, for Kristal it was not until almost two months of being at the Hospital that God Brought forth the complete healing of her daughter, this she confirmed to my wife that it was exactly the way God Said it would happen.

I also remember this couple, the only couple I prayed for at the Hospital, all the other parents were only the mother of the child, this is something that fathers have got to start working on, it's good to be a Father, it is more excellent to become a Dad. I remembered praying for this couple for the healing of their son, and The Lord Told me to ask them if they believed that God was Able to Do this Healing for their child, of which they both agreed that they believed, The Lord Pronounced Healing for their child without any conditions, after the prayer they agreed for themselves without The Lord Forcing them to give their lives over to God, and promised to get Married and Serve The Living God.

Imagine, my son was the main reason for me to be at that Hospital, and I never needed to pray for my son because his sickness was to get me in an environment that The Lord Needed me to be in so that God Could Speak to some Parents and Heal their Children, what A God of Mystery.

The mother of the child that did the surgery kept her promise to God, she is now Baptized and Serving God, she keeps in touch with my wife and the child is as healthy as any normal child. When she got The Word from God she wanted to know if it is that she must now come to my Church to be saved, I told her that was not necessary, if she was closer to my Church that would be good, but seeing that she is two parishes away from where I worshiped I told her to find a Church with The Revelation of Jesus Christ Being God and that will do just fine. What A Mighty God We Serve.

There was a time I was coming from Church having completed one of our Wednesday's Fasting, I was alone in The car, when I was now at the community of Sandy Bay before entering the Scheme for my home, I heard The Voice of Lord Spoke to me, and The Voice Brought forth also The conformation of The Presence of God and also A Vision of a person The Lord Was Directing me to go and Pray for. The Lord Showed me a picture of a young lady that has a store in The community of Sandy Bay that is always at her store selling products, The Lord Said:

"I Need you to find this person and Pray for this person"!

I said to The Lord, but I don't know this person, I only see this person while I'm on the road driving going to Church and coming back from Church. The Lord Responded with an even stronger Anointing that allows goose pimples to fill my whole body, at this time I have already past the place where this person operates her business and The Lord Spoke Again and Said:

"I Need you to find this person and Pray for this person"!

I had to make an immediate U-Turn, safely I must add. I said Yes Lord, I will do what You Have Instructed for me to do! I wasn't interested in finding out what God Would Do if He Spoke to me a third time. I drove to the place that I know was the location that the person had her business, when I got there the business was closed, I asked the person that had a store next to this person's business if she knew the person for the business and where could I find that person, I never even knew the name of that person. The person said to me that she locked up early and went home, and of course this person could not tell me where this person lives because she did not know. I returned to my car and said Lord I can't find the person that You Asked me to Pray for. Upon driving home again, The Anointing of The Lord was still over my body. I decided that I was going to stop at a well known store that everyone in the community knows and investigate if I could find where this person lives. I asked the store owner if she knew the person that operates a business at the front and I gave her the exact location, the store owner said yes she know the person, I asked her If she could direct me to where this person lives, the store owner asked me what was the problem and why I needed to find out where she lives? I told her that I was coming from Fasting and The Lord Showed me her picture and told me to find her and Pray for her. The store owner confirmed and said, yes, God is Good, Yes, this is God! She needs the prayer because she has not been well for a while. She then gave me directions to this person's home.

When I drove to the exact location based on the directions that I got, when I came out the car and called the name that the store owner gave me for the person, I saw four children came out of the house with the eldest one being sensible enough to tell me that her mother is not there, she is gone to the Doctor, I said Lord, why is this person so hard to find, because at that moment it would have been over half of an hour I'm seeking to find this person. I asked the eldest child if she could give me her mother's number, she immediately spoke the number as it was on speed dial in her head, I told her to repeat the number to make certain that I got the right number. I then called the number for the person and finally I was speaking to the person The Lord Told me to find. I said to the person:

"Hello, good evening, I'm here to tell you something strange, I am a Pastor, I don't know you and you do not know me, but The Lord Told me today while I was coming from Fasting

**to find you and pray for you, the person responded by
shouting out to The Lord: Jesus Christ, Thank You Father"!**

**The person said to me, where are you now!
I said I'm at your home.
The person said to me: Don't leave, I'm coming home now!**

I asked the person where she was, she told me that she was in Old Harbour at a Doctor's Office waiting to see a Doctor, I told her that I was going home to get two more person to come and pray with me for her to get healed, the person again cried out in the phone and said don't leave I coming home right now, don't leave because I need the prayer and I've been Praying to God to send someone to pray for me! I told her that I would stay and wait until she came home. I waited another half an hour, then I saw her turn the corner, and immediately she cried out Thank You Jesus Christ! She then came near and said:

**"Garry! How you mean you don't know mi! Are you
not the grandson of Bishop Whitfield? We both grew
up in the same Sunday School! I am such a person
granddaughter and my God-mother is such a person"!**

When she told me those things I began to put a picture to her face and realized that I saw this person before while being young. She then began to tell me that she was praying to God for a while, as it is that she has been sick for over three months, and moving from Doctor to Doctor and spending a whole lot of money and doing a whole lot of test, and not being able to go to work to earn the money to maintain the Doctor's Bill. I told her that The Lord Anointed me to come and pray for her, and not to worry because once God Has Anointed me for the Purpose she will get better. We entered her home with her and her children and we had a Prayer Meeting and read two Psalms, I then Prayed for her and while Praying The Lord Told me to Pray for her Back, so I did. After the Prayer The Lord Said it is done, and gave me some instructions that I must give to her to follow, one of those instructions was an immediate instruction that needed to be carried out the next day so that the spirit's power will be broken from continuing to plague her life, she agreed to all that was Instructed. I told her to call me if she felt sick again and also to let me know her progress, then I left and went home. To God Be The Glory. She called me the next morning to let me know that God is Good, she woke up for the first time out of her bed in a long time and not having any pains, she then told me that when she went outside her home and she saw on the clothes line a Dress that she has been looking for over the past three months, and suddenly after the Prayer, the next day the dress reappears, I told her not to wear that dress but to be discipline enough to burn that dress. To God Be The Glory, this experience took place over three years and the young lady never needed to call me back to pray for her because God Anointed me to Pray for her that she would be made whole. While going to Church daily she is always looking out for me to give me a wave, she also received my first Book called God Steps In. What A Wonderful God.

Again there was this time that I went to my bed this being a Tuesday night because I remembered the next day being a fasting day, while sleeping I heard this number being repeated in my head and just kept on singing that I had to get up and go in the Kitchen with sleep still in my eyes just to write down the number that I heard repeating in my sleep, my wife also got up and asked me what was the matter, I showed her the number that kept repeating in my head while sleeping, she looked on it and said this looks like it is a person's phone number because of the seven digits, she asked me what am I going to do with the number, I said right now I going back to my bed and tomorrow I will pray about that number. I went back to bed and finally was able to sleep, I got up the morning and had a look on the number and realized that this was indeed a person's phone number, I went to Fasting and told The Church about my experience however I never decided what I was going to do with the number, I came back home and my wife asked me if I wasn't going to call the number, I asked what she taught, she said she believes that someone on the other side of this number needs help, and this is God's Way of letting you know that this person needs Prayer. I then decided to call the number, a lady answered and I said:

"Good evening, I do not know you, and you do not know me, but I was given this number while in my sleep last night, are you the owner of this phone number"?

The lady said no, the phone belongs to her husband. I told her that I am a Pastor and would like to speak to her husband. She began to get emotional on the phone and said: O my God, this is not real! She asked me: When did you say you got the number, I said last night about 11:30 PM. The lady said to me that this is not real, too good to be true, this must be God! She then told me that she and her husband were praying in that time period last night asking God to Help them because they have been suffering demonic attacks within their home and at work. I told her that all will be well because if God Allowed your husband's number to enter my circle then God Has Already Granted The Approval for Prayer to be made for your lives. She then told me that she will call me back because she is going on the road to find him because he's gone to a shop. After waiting for about 15-20 minutes the phone rang and I was now speaking to the person to whom the phone number belongs to that awoke me from sleep. He began to tell me all that his wife previously told me and said this is just unbelievable. I asked him if he believed in God and believed that God Could Deliver him and his wife from what they were facing, he said yes. I prayed for him and his wife and children on the phone and also instructed him on what to do next. I told him to find a Church with The Revelation of Jesus Christ Being God and go to that Church and all will be well. To God Be All The Glory Great Things He Continues to Perform in strange ways.

And again there was a time I received a call from someone I knew to look at a vehicle for repair or may have the chance to purchase the vehicle or items on the vehicle if the customer is willing to sell. Now this experience will encourage everyone that is Serving The True and Living God to know that when you're Anointed there is nothing that can cancel your Appointment for The Service of God. When I reached the location of where the vehicle was, the owner of the vehicle opened the gate so that I could drive in with my vehicle, and told me that the vehicle is around the back of the house therefore I can drive all the way around the back to have a look at the vehicle. While driving to the back of the house the front gate was being secured by the owner, I thought nothing of if, it was when I reached the back of the house and got out the vehicle to have a look at the vehicle that I'm schedule to have a look on, I then discovered about five men got up with gun in their hands approaching me and then the owner came around and said:

"This one is ok, looking at him I know there is something about this person"!

I had a look at the vehicle. The owner let me know that I must be careful of where I go because many people who you think are your friend are not looking out for your benefit. I discerned what he was saying and departed immediately.

This experience brought back a memory in my mind when there was this Officer who told me that he could have killed me regarding an incident that never had to reach where it reached. I said to that Officer that people who are given the license to kill me could not do so, and you being a person under the law of the land think that you can do what they could not do seeing that they are not bound to any laws of the land?

We are Anointed for God's Purpose, this does not mean that we are going to be stupid, we must always seek to follow The Movement of The Wave of The Spirit of God, because anywhere The Spirit of God Leads us, it is without doubt that His Spirit is Fully Capable to Protect us from every plans of the enemy.

I met someone about a year ago, a person I know well, and the person said to me that whenever my name is mentioned to get certain work and opportunity to come my way, there is always someone there to tell a lie on me so that I will not receive the opportunity to receive that job; but the person said:

"No matter how they try to bury you, whenever I see you, you're always surviving, those who God Has Bless no man can curse".

For those of us who are Serving The Living God, Take care of The Holy Ghost, it is Given to Protect us, if your Soul which is in direct connection with The Holy Ghost is not in Agreement with an Activity that your schedule to perform, light bulb people of God, there is nothing wrong with you, there is rather something wrong with what you are schedule to perform, and I'm not talking about something that is bad because The Holy Ghost will not be in agreement with anything that moves away from God's Will Being Done. But it is found that there will always be Traps for those who are Serving The True and Living God, because it's always a challenge for the devil to seek to fix traps within the lives of those who are for The Purpose of The Kingdom.

"You Have Been Warned"!

I've found to be a different person around different people that I have encountered with, this is not me, but rather The Spirit of God that lives in me. I'm channeled with a great sense of The Spirit of God to Feel The Environment, if you're not good, I will know; if you're possessed with spirits and demons I'm also going to know because The Holy Ghost Reveals Everything, and there is nothing that can hide from The Spirit of God. If You're a good person I will behave myself in a good manner, if you're found to be a temple that is possessed by demons and spirits, then you can't expect me to behave the way I would behave around a good person in the environment and presence of demons.

Learn this: Demons and evil spirits have one job and that job description has never changed from beginning to end, and the job of spirits and demons is to always **FEED**. If you're a Child of God that has The Anointing of God, you will discover that The Anointing of God Is Always Activated within you're Temple to Block or to Stop spirits and Demons from Feeding, thus possessing another vessel to have Authority over that person for the main purpose to continue the **FEEDING**. This Revelation was Revealed to me by my Father, and I Trust What God Tells me.

To The God of Divine Intelligence, Jesus Christ The Lamb of God, to Him Be All Glory, Honor, Praise and Credits. I Hope there was something to take from this Message to be of Assistance to the lives of God's People. From The Ministry of The Church of Jesus Christ Fellowship, Savannah Cross, Jamaica, West Indies. God's Blessings Always. Pastor Lerone Dinnall.

The Hidden Things...

MANKIND'S GREATEST DECEPTION AND WEAKNESS IS NOT SIN BUT RATHER THE CONFESSION OF THAT SIN TO GOD.

Message # 123

Date Started May 18, 2019
Date Finalized May 18, 2019.

Genesis Chapter 3:6-10.

"And when the woman saw that the tree was good for food, and that it was pleasant to the eyes, and a tree to be desired to make one wise, she took of the fruit thereof, and did eat; and gave also unto her husband with her; and he did eat. And the eyes of them both were opened, and they knew that they were naked; and they sewed fig leaves together, and made themselves aprons. And they heard The Voice of The Lord God Walking in the garden in the cool of the day: <u>and Adam and his wife HID themselves from The Presence of The Lord God amongst the trees of the garden</u>. And The Lord God Called unto Adam, and Said unto him, Where Art

Thou? And he said, I heard Thy Voice in the garden, and I was AFRAID, because I was naked; and I Hid myself".

To The Most Excellent Father Be All Glory, Honor and Praise Forever and Ever, Amen. I'm again Honored to be in this Position that God Can Use me as an Instrument for His Glory. I'm often speaking to The Church and The Minister's Aid of The Church that apart from being separated to receive of God's Revelation, I also find that what works to Receive Revelations from God is for a servant of God to not only be Separated for God's Glory, but also while being Separated to find yourself in Water, whether by going to the Sea or River or taking a Shower or doing some laundry or cleaning the kitchen or washing the Car; whatever a Child of God can do while being Separated that includes **WATER**, that Child of God will be Amazed to Hear what God Now Reveals.

I asked The Lord why is this so, The Lord Response was to ask me if I've ever considered why it is that it's only The Element of Water that is Used to perform The modern day Baptism that grants approval for The Holy Ghost to be Received. The Lord Reveals that water is the cleanest and purest element that can be used to Separate an individual from the Physical life of spirits and enables them to get closer to The Spiritual life, and water is thus used for Baptism because while the person that is in the process of Baptism is fully submerge from the Physical life, whenever it is repeated the words which represents The Key for the approval of Baptism while that person is submerge from the physical life of spirits, then within The Spiritual, Access would have been Granted for that person to receive of the mercies of Saving Grace. Thus this person arises from the water A New person because the water along with The Access words which Represents The Only Key for Saving Grace would have combined to now separate the spirits of the old man from the Body of The New Man, thus it is seen that such an individual will now walk in The Newness of Life if it is that such a person is now determined to follow in The Requirements and Training of The Spirit of God.

The Only Key for Baptism Given by Scripture and through Revelation from God is The Name of Jesus Christ, because The Name of Jesus Christ Fills Father and Father Fills Jesus Christ, it Fills Son and Son Is Jesus Christ and also Jesus Christ Fills The Gift of The Holy Ghost and The Holy Ghost Must Testify that Jesus Christ Is God, as it is, The Holy Ghost Renews a man Physical life to become the Characteristics of The Life that Jesus Christ Pattern for God.

Acts Chapter 2:37-41.

"Now when they heard this, they were pricked in their heart, and said unto Peter and to the rest of the Apostles, Men and brethren, what shall we do? Then Peter said unto them, <u>Repent, and be Baptized every one of you in The Name of Jesus Christ for the remission of sins, and ye shall receive The Gift of The Holy Ghost.</u>

(This Represents The Doctrine of God's Ministry for Salvation).

For the Promise is unto you, and to your children, and to all that are afar off, even as many as The Lord our God Shall Call. And with many other words did he Testify and Exhort, saying, Save yourselves from this untoward generation. Then they that gladly received his word were Baptized: and the same day there were added unto them about three thousand souls".

Acts Chapter 8:35-40.

"Then Philip opened his mouth, and began at the same scripture, and preached unto him Jesus. And as they went on their way, they came unto a certain WATER: and the Eunuch said, See, here is water, what doth hinder me to be Baptized? <u>And Philip said, If thou Believest with all thine heart,</u>

thou mayest. And he answered and said, I believe that Jesus Christ is The Son of God. and he commanded the chariot to stand still: and they went down both into the water, both Philip and the Eunuch; and he Baptized him. And when they were come up out of the water, The Spirit of The Lord Caught Away Philip, that the Eunuch saw him no more: and he went on his way rejoicing. But Philip was found at Azotus: and passing through he preached in all the cities, till he came to Caesarea".

Acts Chapter 10:34-48. Verse 42-48 Says:

"And He Commanded us to preach unto the people, and to testify that it is He which was Ordained of God to be The Judge of Quick and Dead. To Him give all the prophets witness, that through His Name whosoever believeth in Him Shall Receive Remission of Sins. While Peter yet spake these words, The Holy Ghost Fell on all them which heard the Word. And they of the circumcision which believeth were astonished, as many as came with Peter, because that on the Gentiles also was poured out The Gift of The Holy Ghost. For they heard them speak in Tongues, and Magnify God. Then answered Peter, Can any man Forbid WATER, that these should not be Baptized, which have received The Holy Ghost as well as we? And he commanded them to be Baptized in The Name of The Lord. Then prayed they him to tarry certain days".

I've seen people receive The Gift of The Holy Ghost even before Baptism, but still this event confirmed within them that they must now be Baptized of which they did. It must be understood that God Would Not Have Given The Gift of The Holy Ghost if He had not already Seen that such a person will become 100% Obedient to The Operation of The Holy Ghost to now confirm that Baptism must be carried out in The Name of Jesus Christ.

Acts Chapter 19:1-7.

"And it came to pass, that, while Apollos was at Corinth, Paul having passed through the upper coasts came to Ephesus: and finding certain Disciples, He said unto them, Have ye received The Holy Ghost since ye believed? And they said unto him, We have not so much as heard whether there be any Holy Ghost. And he said unto them, Unto what then were ye Baptized? And they said, Unto John's Baptism. Then said Paul, John verily Baptized with the Baptism of repentance, saying unto the people, that they should believe on Him which should come after him, that is, on Christ Jesus. When they heard this, they were Baptized in The Name of The Lord Jesus. And when Paul had laid his hands upon them, The Holy Ghost Came on them; and they spake with tongues, and prophesied. And all the men were about twelve".

A Pastor spoke to me on a certain day when I was invited by that Pastor at their Church, and there was within the mind of that Pastor a great concern regarding the young people of the Church not remaining saved; no matter what is done the youths are not staying in the Church, I told the Pastor that we have to pray more often for the youths of the Church that God will have His Way in their lives.

This was the Physical me speaking, the Physical way of looking at what was put before me to give a suggestion.

I was asked to be one of the Speakers at that meeting, I accepted and asked The Lord to be my Guide. While Preaching and Teaching because I find myself doing both whenever I'm called to do something for God, The Lord Opened my eyes and allowed The Spiritual man to speak to that Pastor within the Pulpit, and this was what The Lord Said:

"Those who are given the permission to Baptize people, Are they Anointed by My Spirit to do so? If The person that

is doing the Baptism is not Anointed By God to Perform Baptism, then those who are being Baptized will never realize or experience The Birth of A New Life because the person who acts in that capacity as a Mediator for Baptism does not have the touch of A New Life Experience to usher another person into A New Life's Experience"!

Now when these Words came out of my mouth I almost put my hands over my mouth, because it was then I believed I was being disrespectful to a Pastor, however when I was finish Preaching, the Pastor came to me and said:

"When The Lord Allowed you to speak those words I felt the Burning, and I knew that was the Answer".

This Pastor is a woman therefore she allows others within her Church to perform Baptism.

We are taught through the Stories within The Bible that the devil is always making petitions for our lives before The Presence of God. Now it is seen through the Story of Job that we don't have to do something wrong or within the wrong line of life for God to Grant the Approval for the enemy to have their desire within our lives, but this Approval will always be Granted to thus prove to ourselves, prove to the devil and also confirm that which God Already Knows about us, and this is **FIXED**, there is nothing we can do about it.

I explained in one of my Messages that The Lord Allowed me to Understand that the Test is only set for those who are Children of God, therefore A Child of God should never look at another person's life and wonder why it is that they are not facing what you are facing in life. A Child of God is Marked, Stamped, Labeled for The Test; everyone else is Destined for The Eternal Stress and Fire.

It is however seen that a Child of God Inner man can be comfortable during any Test because that Child of God would have understood the real meaning of Relationship with The Father. What this means is that everything that we do whether it be Good or Bad, especially if it resembles the action of sin, then the first person to know about that sin would be the Only Person that is Able to remove that sin and cast it into the Sea of forgetfulness. Therefore, whenever the devil is making petitions for something to happen within our lives, let it not be because there is found within us Unforgiven Sins or Unconfessed Sins, but rather, let the Test comes our way because our Father Needs to Boost in us for what He Already Knows He Has Put Within us.

I asked myself this Question many times and also asked The Church to look into it, this is the Question: What would have happened if Adam and Eve, the moment they discovered that they have Sinned; What would have happened if they both acknowledge that they have sinned, instead of God Searching for them to tell them that they have Sin?_____.

I Know the punishment would still be death from The Spiritual because God Already Told them that this would be the Reaction of Sin, but it leaves a gap in our minds to just consider the Possibilities of what God Could Have Done to lighten the load of the sin that was committed.

David was a man after God's Own Heart because everything that happened to David God Knew that He Would Get The Truth, therefore, while David received Punishment because of sin, it never cost him Spiritual Death for himself and his Generation. King Saul was a man Rejected by God because he decided that he could hide the truth from God, thus resulting in Spiritual Death for himself and his generation before The Presence of God.

Think about this: When we sin and are Truthful to God in every Action under the Sun, then when the devil goes to make petitions to destroy our Souls for the wrongs which we have done, Can we just View within The Spiritual that God Is Saying to The devil:

"I Know My Servant Committed Fornication or Adultery or Stealing or Lying etc. Because has it happened, my servant was on his knees begging Me for Forgiveness, and have Repented of those Sins, therefore those Sins I've Forgotten about, and it is now in The Sea of Forgetfulness, thus permission is denied".

I need my Readers to understand that Being and Remaining a Christian comes with Spiritual Clarity, let us not accept this World's teaching to believe that the best thing to do when something goes wrong within our lives is to keep it a secret and hide it under the carpet.

Question: Is it really a secret if God Knows about it?_____.
Then why do we seek to hide it, when The Lord Said that the Night and the Day are both alike unto Him?_____.

Let God Be **TRUTH** and every man a Liar. If our Destination and Home is in Heaven, then we must be Born in the Understanding that the only way to get there is **TRUTH UNTO THE FATHER OF TRUTH!** If we are living in Sin and Lies and Deceptions, Wake up! That's the Wrong Foundation, A Weak Foundation Must **SINK!**

I Hope this Message would have reached the persons that it should bring encouragement to, thus Establishing God's Will Being Done in Our Lives. To The Most Excellent Father Be All Credits, Honor, Praise, Forever and Ever. From The Ministry of The Church of Jesus Christ Fellowship Savannah Cross, Jamaica, West Indies. Pastor Lerone Dinnall, God Bless.

Putting The Truth Before God Is Always The Best Option!

PHASE THREE

**The Closing;
The Divine Prophecies from The Speech
of The Holy Ghost... The First Divine Step
or Access within The Authority of God.**

I AM DOING A NEW THING, SAITH THE LORD!

Message # 104   Date Started January 10, 2019
                             Date Finalized January 10, 2019.

Number Chapter 23:19.

"God Is not a man, that He should lie; neither the son of man, that He should repent: hath He Said, and shall He Not Do It? or hath He Spoken, and shall He Not Make It Good"?

To The God of All Secrets, Mysteries and Wonders, to Him Be All Glory, Honor and Praise; to Jesus Christ The Lamb of God. I'm Privileged again to find myself in this Position that I can be God's Available Instrument. Let's Get to it.

I Received A Vision on the 24 th of December 2018, but never found the time to write down the Vision until now. I however called My Grandmother in New Jersey and told her about the Vision that I had received from God. The Vision is as Follows:

I was brought to a Church in My Vision, of which there was a Pastor in The Pulpit, bringing forth the Sermon that he had prepared. I don't know The Church nor do I know the Pastor, but if I was to see the Pastor again, I would no doubt be able to acknowledge that, that was the Pastor I saw in My Vision. While the Pastor was Preaching to the congregation, The Presence of God Came Down and Rested on The Pastor, it can be explained to that which happened to Jesus Christ when He first got Baptized, The Spirit of God Came down like A Dove. So it was in The Vision, The Pastor was Preaching, and The Presence of God Came Down in The Church and Rested upon The Pastor and The Pastor Immediately began to Break Down with Real Tears, and Changed the Focus of his Topic and began to Repent in The Pulpit, he began to explain to his Congregation that God Required him to Speak in The Direction of Repentance, and there was nothing he could do about it because he was being reprimanded by The Presence of The Almighty God. I Heard A Voice Spoke to me and Said:

"I AM DOING A NEW THING, LET THEM GO AND PREACH AND I WILL PUT THEM ON MY SCALE, THUS SAITH THE LORD".

That's The Vision, I Hope that we will Discern what The Vision is Revealing, In The Mighty Name of Jesus Christ.

God is considered to be Slow, but there is one certainty, God Is Sure. I Remember in the year 2014, I got numerous Visions of God Commanding me to Build an Altar, when I was finally convinced, The Word of The Lord Came to me and Said:

"A Call For Holiness, Get Back To Holiness".

The Lord Assured me that this was the season The Church should be Focused on, because He's Going to Shake The Heavens, He's Going to Shake The Earth, The Sea, The Hills and all People upon the Land.

I've almost reached four years in Ministry, and I've Observed that God Was Ready a long time ago to do the Shaking from the moment He Spoke those Words out of His Mouth, but His People was not yet Measured up to the Required Level of Holiness that will see them being Protected from that which is to come upon the Land.

For those that have not yet noticed The Signs of The Almighty, Wake Up and Stop from Sleeping! God Is Doing A New Thing, and that New Operation must begin with The Church. If The Church cannot and will not find Itself to Be Holy, Then The Church is in Trouble, because God Is No Respecter of Persons.

Let's End With Prayer…

Father of Heaven and Earth, I Honor Your Mighty Name Jesus Christ, I Pray that You Will Forgive Your People of Our Sins, has we Confess to You that we have Sinned, Our Forefathers Have Sinned and it is certain that our Children will Sin. We Acknowledge Lord that we have come short of Your Requirements, even in Church, and we Ask You Father to Help Your People to Measure up to The Requirements of Holiness. Lord, we need to be a part of The Saints when it's time to March into Glory, and we Know that this will not be Possible if we have not Measured up to Your Requirements. Father, we Pray In The Name of Jesus Christ that You Will Continue to Lead and Direct our Paths, because we cannot Direct our own Lives. This we Ask in The Saving Name of Jesus Christ, Amen.

We Thank The Lord for Live Visions, that will help to direct the lives of those who are to escape what is to come, in The Name of Jesus Christ we Give Thanks. From The Ministry of The Church of Jesus Christ Fellowship, Savannah Cross, Jamaica, West Indies. Pastor Lerone Dinnall.

**Be Ye Holy, For I AM HOLY.
Let Us Start With Trying, Then It Will
Manifest To Become A Discipline.**

INTELLIGENCE MEETS DIVINE INTELLIGENCE!

Message # 167   Date Started December 14, 2020
Date Finalized December 14, 2020.

"The Lord Speaketh"

Thus Saith The Lord, for those who hide in the dark and maketh decisions to cement the path of life, I Seeth Thee, makest thyself to be a god, gathering information from all your sources to conclude that which must now be life's event and life's direction, I Seeth thee.

Knowest thou not that great responsibilities becometh great care and to him that increaseth in much knowledge is a burden to that man which wears that mantle. But thou as made thyself to be a god and there is no god beside Me, I Know not any.

Because thou art in this position of intelligence and abused thy responsibilities and maketh things to flow in the direction in which you being a god so disereth it to be which is not of Me, I Say Curse, I Say Curse, I Say A Curse shall never leave thee, thou who makest thyself to be a god.

intelligence without Me be A Curse, let thy life be A Curse, let thy children be A Curse, let everything you will ever put your hands to be A Curse and it will remain being A Curse because I The Divine Intelligence have called it to be A Curse.

I Will put a mark upon intelligence that have made themselves to be a god, a mark just as how I placed a mark on Cain, a mark because thou thinkest that thou has intelligence above Me. Sealed, It Is Sealed, It Is Sealed.

Not one word that is spoken against those who serve me will never go unpunished, I have marked those words and I have marked those persons, Sealed, It Is Sealed, It Is Sealed, it will not go unpunished.

Those who look down upon My Church, Fear is coming, I knoweth your fear and I will increase your fears then I Will Allow that which you fear to be realized because I Am God That Can Do It.

For those who says they will never be broke again and have not made certain that they were gathering riches by My Hands, Learn, when will you Learn, If it is not By Me and From Me then you can never be rich because I The Lord God Almighty Did Not Make you to be rich.

I Planted The Mountains and it cannot be moved for the time that I Have Planted it to be there, I Have Made The Valley, I Designed The Sea, The Heaven Is My Dwelling and I Stand Upon The Earth. Fear Me Because I Alone can Plant, I Alone Bringeth The Increase and I Alone Set It Fixed for all times to Stand in The Position that I have Declared and Decreed for it to stand in. I Am God, I Make Rich and I Maketh poor.

Curse Is he that bringeth and continue to bring a false report against those who trust in Me and fear My Name, I Say Again Curse be any man which speaketh and maketh a Lie against My

Inheritance, The Curse shall never leave your children, Sealed, It Is Sealed, It is Sealed.

Curse be him that despises My Word, make your own words and see for yourself which words shall stand, My Words Will Never go Tired and it will never Sleep because I and My Words are One In Eternity.

I Shall Break the altars of the physicians that keep My People Oppressed to make themselves fat, again I Say that a man can never be rich unless that man is found linked to The CONTINUATION of All Things Which Was, Which Is and Which Is To Come, The Almighty.

I Need True Teacher to Train the generation which is to come in My Will, I Shall Sieve, I Will Remove, I Will Cast away The Teachers of the Strange gods from The generation that shall have no number, Sealed, It is Sealed, It is Sealed.

I Shall Be Feared, I Will Be Feared, I Must Be Feared, I Am The Almighty and It's My Time To Gather My Tithes. Sealed, It Is Sealed, It Is Sealed. Thus Saith The Lord.

I will Direct my readers to The Spirit of True Intelligence, Jesus Christ, to Him Be All Glory, Honor and Praise. From Pastor Lerone Dinnall and The Ministry of The Church of Jesus Christ Fellowship, Savannah Cross, Jamaica, West Indies. Take it or leave it, Freewill.

Divine Intelligence Has Spoken, The Wise Will Listen And Prepare!

THE LORD VISITS!

Message # 95

Date Started May 5, 2018
Date Finalized May 5, 2018.

Psalms 14.

"The Fool hath said in his heart, there is no God. They are
corrupt, they have done abominable works, there is none that
doeth good. The Lord looked down from heaven upon the
children of men, to see if there were any that did understand,
and seek God. They are all gone aside, they are all together
become filthy: there is none that doeth good, no, not one.
Have all the workers of iniquity no knowledge? Who eat up
my people as they eat bread, and call not upon The Lord.
There were they in great fear: for God is in the generation of
the righteous. Ye have shamed the council of the poor, because
The Lord is his refuge. Oh that the Salvation of Israel were
come out of Zion! When The Lord Bringeth Back the captivity
of his people, Jacob shall rejoice, and Israel shall be Glad".

Greeting to all God's Wonderful People, Receive Greetings in The
Mighty Name of Jesus Christ our Soon Coming King. I'm Privileged
again to be God's Pen and Mouth; however, this is a Message I wished
I was not the person writing; but I remain to be God's Instrument;
Humble and Willing I must remain. Let's get to The Message at hand.

About three Months ago I received A Vision from God that I never
put down on paper, because of how terrifying The Vision was; I how-

ever wrote down what I saw on What's App, and sent it to those who I could send it to. The Vision is as follows:

I saw buildings of employment, not one or two, but a whole lot of buildings; these buildings were being destroyed because the Earth opened her mouth to sink these buildings; a lot of people died, but there were a few that lived to tell the tale. It was complete destruction. At the end of The Vision The Lord Said:

"They Have removed The Righteous from their Positions in Business and have put their friends, therefore these buildings could not stand, because The Righteous are The Spiritual Steel that holds each place of business together".

This was The Vision three months ago. Now on the second of May 2018, we were at The Church observing our Divine Complete Fasting. Now this is a Fast that we ask all members of The Church to be a part of, it takes place every first Wednesday for every month, and the Goal is to bring all family members to this Fasting service for A Divine Deliverance; it is The Church Standard by God's Command to start this type of Fasting 6pm on Tuesday evening and continue into Wednesday, and so it was observed. On this day The Church had a particular Topic that we were looking on; while the Topic was being observed by the members of The Church, I sat in The Church and was carried into the same Vision I had received from The Lord Three months ago, at the end of the Vision The Lord Said:

"This Is Going To Happen".

The Lord Revealed to me a Scripture in The Book of Genesis Chapter 18; when it is that The Lord Came down to Observed for Himself if the type of wickedness that was being done in Sodom and Gomorra was actually True; of which Abraham Intercede with God for the people. God Agreed that if He found Ten people in the city that was Righteous, He would not Destroy the City; it turns out that God Could Not Find the Ten Righteous, therefore the City was Destroyed.

The Lord Revealed to me on Wednesday Fasting Day, that He is going to Walk on the Land to See for Himself; and that which The Lord Said He's Seeking for, is to Identify where they have placed The Righteous; The Lord Said, He's Seeking for at least 10% of Righteous in everything that speaks to Business and also Place of Worship, because Judgment begin in The House of God. The Lord Revealed that if there is not found the 10% of Righteous People, then The Church and Business will not Stand, because it is written:

"The Righteous Must Inherit The Earth".

I don't know if all this is going to take place in a Day, what I do know is that The Lord is going to Walk Through every establishment of Worship First, and if it is found that His House is not Acceptable, then that place of Worship will not be Able Stand. And who can stop God!

The Lord Reveals that the next place to be Judged is The House of Justice, those who make laws to keep the Rich richer and to keeps the poor with chains around their necks; those who call Evil good and good evil; that put darkness for light, and light for darkness; that put bitter for sweet, and sweet for bitter. Isaiah Chapter 5: 20-25. After this The Lord Reveals that Every Place of Business will be put on His Scale, to identify where they have placed The Righteous. The Lord Reveals that He Has Heard The Cry of The Righteous; and He Is Coming to FIX The Righteous in their Positions and Possessions and no man can stop God, Because there must be A Generation of Righteousness to continue until the end. That's the Vision.

I Shared this with other Pastors, and they also have received similar Message from God; and we've come to the acknowledgement that The Righteous Saints all over need to now be in constant Prayer, at all times, because we will be experiencing some type of disasters from The Hand of God.

Question: Can this type of Disaster Be Stopped? Yes it can! But it is going to require Repentance, it is going to require a Change of heart of how we Worship The Father in Spirit and in Truth Firstly; then it is going to require a Change in the Directions of how Laws are made for this Country; It is going to require for those in Business to put Righteous People in Positions thus ensuring that there is a continual Acceptance from The Lord to Keep those Businesses going. Truth be told it is going to require Change.

Is it impossible? The King of Nineveh heard that in forty days Nineveh shall be destroyed, and he commanded Change for his kingdom, that saw God Repenting of what He was going to Do. Jonah Chapter 3.

Can this Disaster Be Stopped? Let us see what we do Next as a Country.

For The Righteous that is Serving God in Spirit and in Truth, let us get Deeper in God; let us Continue in Fasting, Pray without ceasing, because The Lord Is Going to Walk on the Land, I know not when, but The Lord Said it is going to Happen. And I received this Message in Fasting, Believe or don't Believe, Free Will. As for me and my house, we will Serve The Lord. Pastor Lerone Dinnall. The Ministry of The Church of Jesus Christ Fellowship.

The Lord Visits!

SEPARATION, THE KEY!

Message # 166 Date Started December 14, 2020
Date Finalized December 14, 2020.

Genesis Chapter 12:1-3.

"Now The Lord had Said unto Abram, Get Thee out of thy country, and from thy kindred, and from thy father's house, unto a land that I Will Shew Thee: And I Will Make of thee a great nation, and I Will Bless thee, and make thy name great; and thou shalt be a blessing: And I Will Bless them that bless thee, and curse him that curseth thee: and in thee shall all families of the earth be blessed".

Greetings again Royal People of God in The Only Matchless Name of Jesus Christ, it is an Honor to find myself in a position of Heaven's Worth to please The Father first and then to edify The Family of God. I've often found myself Teaching The People of God about this Scripture to make reference to the Saints that God was identifying to His People, one of the Foundational Ingredients that must be furnished within the life of any believer in order to receive that which is their Divine Blessing from The Father. That foundational value is called **SEPARATION**. God Needed to Bless Abram but is always found Jealous of where His Divine Blessing goes to and for whom that Divine Blessing will remain on for the rest of their lives and for the lives of their generations to continue living in.

I Taught The Church this Fact: God Needed to Bless Abram but God could not Bless Abram in his current environment. It is first identified that Abram was separated within The Spiritual first, which is his mind, then that manifestation of Spiritual gave birth to the manifestation of the physical which was to move on to that which the Spiritual have identified to be a must travel for The Divine Blessings of that which is promised by God. There are many times a believer will receive that which God had promised and have kept that which God has promised to them for a long time, but Receiving without Movement of the physical is not Accepting from God that which is first received from The Spiritual. Many Saints can acknowledge that they have received which is also known as The Declared Word, but many have not yet understood that The Declared Word of God is not the same as The Decreed Word of God, yes, it is tied to each other but the distances between both always spells the word in the physical that which is called **TIME**.

God Always has to make known what He Is about to do to thus fulfill that Speech in His Time and not in man's time. The Official Speech of God is known as The Declared Word, meaning it is just Spoken but not yet fulfilled. The Decreed Word is that which is always manifesting from that which was originally Declared by The Father and it must be directly tied to that which The Father had Originally Spoken out of His Mouth being The Declared Word at first.

God Cannot be measured or traced but there are always Words that are Fixed to allow a Believer to identify what is Declared that will officially lead to that which will be Decreed by The Father. Therefore as I have always said to people that just don't believe in what The Lord Asked me to write, Time will always speak the Truth and furthermore The Lord Says: My Glory Will I Not Give To Another. This simply means that if this was not of God, there would not only be an Angry God Ready to Execute Vengeance but also A Jealous God, meaning, if there is someone using an Authority that belongs to God without His Approval, now that's dangerous!

Many have not yet understood that every speech that is declared from a person to an Authority must be measured. A person will never be able to call on The Approval Filled Name of Jesus Christ without identifying for themselves that This Approval will now Show Up, that's the main reason why many will only use the name jesus because it is just limited and truly has no direction as to who exactly is being called upon, but The people that knows their God, that uses The Authority of The Name Jesus Christ will then Identify that there is absolutely no power that can stand close to The Full Approval of The Name of Jesus Christ.

There are many things that The Lord Needs to Change for the life of a believer but change will never be realized if this believer both Spiritually and physically remains in the same environment. Think about it, The Almighty God Asked Abram to Separate himself for his Divine Blessing which was already in God's Hands but only Fixed for an environment that only God Approves. We know for ourselves that we represent an Altar for God that is Clean, do we know for sure the environment that we associate ourselves with to be of the same material of an Altar like ourselves that will force God's Approval? _____Now that's the main Question to Ask!

Many times a Child of God finds themselves in the company of those who God Needs to destroy but have not yet identified that God Will Never Destroy a place if there is still The Righteous in that place. God Is Seeking to Destroy False Altars but if there is one righteous still present upon that Altar then the Altar will remain for that one righteous. There are many times a Believer is seeking to climb The Spiritual Ladder in God but will never find the steps muchless to see the Ladder to climb if that believer of God is surrounded by those who represent the other gods, **TRUTH**! Take it up with God, He Asked me to write this message! Separation is the key! A Child of God must never find themselves loving their environment more than how they love God and love themselves. A Child of God must be quick to understand that God's Divine Blessing is never limited and also gain the knowledge that whenever God Speaks forth The Divine

Word of Blessing which is Declared upon His Children, it never has an ending because God has no ending which means that if God Blesses a man for Divine Inheritance, The God which Establishes The Past, Maintained The Present and Seals The Future, This same God did not Bless a man and forget about that man's generation. That's The God of Inheritance, No Beginning and no Ending from Eternity to Eternity. Is this your GOD?_____.

If not, then you need to release yourself from the other gods of promises and find The One True and Living God that is never weak, that never goes tired, that always keeps promises and never forgets about our Inheritance, The True God. Power is in the hands of the man who hears The Words of The Lord. This means that no one can change you but you. Someone can pray for you that's good, it's even better if you have done it for yourself, and remember that sincere Prayers must be directed through The Name of Jesus Christ.

Every event in The Bible that The Lord was about to do something it always needed the separation of God's Chosen people from those who were just pretending to be God's People, without separation God Did Nothing but Warn, after separation God Did Great Miracles, brought His People through the red sea and also destroyed those who oppressed His People for years. Separation Is The Key. The moment Lot was separated from Abram his uncle God Poured Divine Approvals on Abram's life.

Genesis Chapter 13:14-18.

"And The Lord Said unto Abram, after that Lot was Separated from him, Lift up now thine eyes, and look from the place where thou art northward, and southward, and eastward, and westward: For all the land which thou seest, to thee will I Give it, and to thy seed for ever. And I Will Make thy seed as the dust of the earth: so that if a man can number the dust of the earth, then shall thy seed also be numbered. Arise,

walk through the land in the length of it and in the breadth of it; for I Will Give it unto thee. Then Abram removed his tent, and came and dwelt in the plain of Mamre, which is in Hebron, and built there an Altar unto The Lord".

Numbers Chapter 16:20-35.

"And The Lord Spake unto Moses and Aaron, Saying, Separate yourself from among this congregation, that I May Consume them in a moment. And they fell upon their faces, and said, O God, The God of The Spirits of all flesh, shall one man sin, and wilt thou be wroth with all the congregation? And The Lord Spake unto Moses, Saying, Speak unto the congregation, saying, Get you up from about the tabernacle of Korah, Dathan, and Abiram. And Moses rose up and went unto Dathan and Abiram; and the elders of Israel followed him. And he spake unto the congregation, saying, Depart, I pray you, from the tents of these wicked men, and touch nothing of their, lest ye be consumed in all their sins. So they gat up from the tabernacle of Korah, Dathan and Abiram, on every side: and Dathan and Abiram came out, and stood in the door of their tents, and their wives, and their sons, and their little children. And Moses said, Hereby ye shall know that The Lord Hath Sent me to do all these works; for I have not done them of mine own mind. If these men die the common death of all men, or if they be visited after the visitation of all men; then The Lord Hath not Sent me. But if The Lord Make A New Thing, and the earth open her mouth, and swallow them up, with all that appertain unto them, and they go down quick into the pit; then ye shall understand that these men have provoked The Lord. And it came to pass, as he had made an end of speaking all these words, that the ground clave asunder that was under them: And the earth opened her mouth, and swallowed them up, and their houses, and all the men that appertained unto Korah, and all their goods. They, and all that appertained to them, went down alive into the pit, and the earth closed upon them: and they perished from among the congregation. And all Israel that were round about them fled at the cry of them: for they said, Lest the earth swallow us up also. And there came out a fire from The Lord, and consumed the two hundred and fifty men that offered incense".

Thus Saith The Lord, I Will Declare The Decree, I Will Do It By My Own Might, I Will Break Down that which is not of Me and I Will Establish and Cause to Remain that which is of Me, Mark My Words Because it is Sealed. Man cannot do that which I Alone Will Do. I Will Cause Fear to Again Be in My House, I Looked Down and there is no fear of GOD, The Church Will Again Fear, The Inhabitants of the Land Will Again Tremble and Fear Me because I Am The Only I Am. It Is Sealed. It Is Sealed. It Is Sealed.

Note: I did not say but rather The Spirit of The Lord Says it is so, I'm just a vessel that The Lord Choose to Use. Let us see, time will tell, time always reveals the Truth. To The God of Speech that both Declares and Decrees and it remains as He Says, In The Name of Jesus Christ, Amen. From Pastor Lerone Dinnall and The Ministry of The Church of Jesus Christ Fellowship, Savannah Cross, Jamaica, West Indies. Believe or don't believe it remains to be a choice, Freewill. God Bless.

Separation Is The Key For Divine Blessing!

WARNING FOR THE BACK TO NORMAL...

Message # 130

Date Started May 3, 2020
Date Finalized May 3, 2020.

Psalms 24.

"The Earth is The Lord's, and the fulness thereof; the world, and they that dwell therein. For He hath Founded it upon the seas, and Established it upon the floods. Who shall ascend into The Hill of The Lord? Or who shall stand in His Holy Place? He that hath clean hands, and a pure heart; who hath not lifted up his soul unto vanity, nor sworn deceitfully. He shall receive the Blessing from The Lord, and righteousness from The God of his salvation. This is the generation of them that seek Him, that seek Thy Face, O Jacob. Lift up your heads, O ye gates; and be ye lift up, ye everlasting doors; and The King of Glory shall Come In. Who Is This King of Glory? The Lord Strong and Mighty, The Lord Mighty in battle. Lift up your heads, O ye gates; even lift them up, ye everlasting doors; and The King of Glory Shall Come In. Who is this King of Glory? The Lord of Hosts. He Is The King of Glory".

To The God of Excellent Timing and Purpose, To Him Be All Glory, Honor and Praise through The Access Name of Jesus Christ.

Here we go again with another Vision from this Pastor, the time is now 1:22 AM, Jamaica time. The Lord Refreshed my thoughts of a Vision that He Gave me in the past and Said:

"It's Time To Let Them Know".

Now before any Church, Government, Business, Country and Nation Accept this Prophecy or Prediction, please go on your knees and Pray, enter into some meaningful Fasting, Seek The Face of God for yourself and ask The Lord if this Prophecy or Prediction from this Pastor is True or is it False and see what God Says…

Let's go…

The Lord Says it's Time to Show My Might, for The Church, The Government, The Nation and Country that Fears Their God To Listen.

The Lord Says…

"When going back to a sense of normal for life the only way forward to Please Me Must be Righteousness and nothing else. The Lord Desires to See The Spiritual Steels in their Rightful Positions in Church and Government and in everything that speaks towards Business for a person to earn. The Lord Says to let it be known that those who are My Spiritual Steel Shall remain in Their Positions; The Lord Requires at least 10% of Spiritual Steels in Church, in Government and also in Business. The Lord Says: Just Test Me and see if that Church, Government and Business will stand if I Don't find 10% of Spiritual Steel. Thus Speaketh The Lord, It Will Not Stand. Thus Saith The Lord, It Will Not Stand. Thus Saith He That Hath All Strength, It Will Not Stand! Seal, It Is Seal, It Is Seal"!

I'm writing this Message and find myself not wanting and desiring to be the person that should write this Message, but when do we have a say in that which God Needs for His Vessels to Fulfill. The Lord Says He Needs for this Message to be Known and to reach the ears of those who it should reach so that they will know that this was Spoken From The Lord, therefore it will now be left to see what direction is now taken from those who have heard what Thus Saith The Lord.

To conclude this Message I will remind those who are reading of what The Vision is. The Lord Revealed A Vision to me about two years ago, I got the vision twice, and The Lord Said it is going to happen. I saw Buildings being swallowed by the earth, not one but a lot of buildings and a whole lot of people died and only a few survived. And within that Vision I asked The Lord Why? And God Said:

"This Happened because they have moved The Righteous out of their Positions in Business and that The Righteous Represents The Spiritual Steel for everything that must be Manifested and remain Manifested, The Lord Said The Righteous have been removed therefore these Building could not stand before Him".

Here is an advice for Churches, Government, Business, Nations and Countries:

- **Leave God's People In Their Positions!**

- **Let it be that they have retired and no longer desire to work, and if they retire, find another Righteous Spiritual Steel to fill the Gap.**

- **Leave The Righteous In Their Position!
It's A Warning, Message Delivered!**

Who knows what is being planned by Churches, Government, Countries, Nations and Businesses of this world, the normal man will never know, but God Knows and God Has Spoken. I'm often telling people that have an hard time believing what God has Shown to me to speak, and this is what I always say to them:

Have you considered that I'm saying that God Says? Now if you read the Bible, if God did not Say, then I'm found to be a Blasphemer, and the last time I checked, I'm Still Saying that God Has Spoken and am still alive, my wife is still alive and also my children and The Church is still Growing from strength to strength with amazing young people that are set to take their rightful place in this life, think about that!

No need to wonder too hard if God Has Spoken, time must tell, and God Never Speaks A Word that He Is Not Prepared To Stand Firm Upon What He Said, Think About That!

I have done that which The Lord Requires me to do, let the world witness that I am free. Unto The King of kings, The God of Unsearchable Understanding, Knowledge and Wisdom through The Only Access Name of Jesus Christ, Amen. Pastor Lerone Dinnall from The Church of Jesus Christ Fellowship, Savannah Cross, Jamaica, West Indies.

God Bless, Preserve and Protect The Righteous, The Spiritual Steel.

Warning For The Back To Normal...

Write Your Personal Revelation From God, Add Your Special Touch To Your Book From This Ministry.

1. _____

2. _____

3. _____

4. _____

5. _____

6. _____

7. _____

8. _____

9. _____

10. _____

11. _____

12. _____

13. _____

14. _____

15. _____

16. _____

17. _____

18. _____

19. _____

20. _____

21. _____

22. _____

23. _____

24. _____

25. _____

CLOSING SCRIPTURES

Psalm 51.

" Have mercy upon me, O God, according to thy lovingkindness: according unto the multitude of thy tender mercies blot out my transgressions. Wash me throughly from mine iniquity, and cleanse me from my sin. For I acknowledge my transgressions: and my sin is ever before me. Against thee, thee only, have I sinned, and done this evil in thy sight: that thou mightest be justified when thou speakest, and be clear when thou judgest. Behold, I was shapen in iniquity; and in sin did my mother conceive me.

Behold, thou desirest truth in the inward parts: and in the hidden part thou shalt make me to know wisdom. Purge me with hyssop, and I shall be clean: wash me, and I shall be whiter than snow. Make me to hear joy and gladness; that the bones which thou hast broken may rejoice. Hide thy face from my sins, and blot out all mine iniquities. Create in me a clean heart, O God; and renew a right spirit within me. Cast me not away from thy presence; and take not thy Holy Spirit from me. Restore unto me the joy of thy salvation; and uphold me with thy free Spirit.

Then will I teach transgressors thy ways; and sinners shall be converted unto thee. Deliver me from bloodguiltiness, O God, thou God of my salvation: and my tongue shall sing aloud of thy righteousness. O Lord, open thou my lips; and my mouth shall shew forth thy praise. For thou desirest not sacrifice; else would I give it: thou delightest not in burnt offering. The sacrifices of God are a broken spirit: a broken and a contrite heart, O God, thou wilt not despise. Do good in thy good pleasure unto Zion:

Build thou the walls of Jerusalem. Then shalt thou be pleased with the sacrifices of righteousness, with burnt offering and whole burnt offering: then shall they offer bullocks upon thine Altar ”.

Jonah Chapter 3

“ And The Word of The Lord came unto Jonah the second time, Saying, Arise, Go unto Nineveh, that great city, and preach unto it the preaching that I bid thee. So Jonah arose, and went unto Nineveh, according to The Word of The Lord. Now Nineveh was an exceeding great city of three days journey. And Jonah began to enter into the city a days journey, and he cried, and said, yet forty days, and Nineveh shall be overthrown. So the people of Nineveh believed God, and proclaimed a fast, and put on sackcloth, from the greatest of them even to the least of them. For word came unto the king of Nineveh, and he arose from his throne, and he laid his robe from him, and covered him with sackcloth, and sat in ashes. And he caused it to be proclaimed and published through Nineveh by the decree of the king and his nobles, saying, Let neither man nor beast, herd nor flock, taste any thing: let them not feed, nor drink water: But let man and beast be covered with sackcloth, and cry mightily unto God: yea, let them turn every one from his evil way, and from the violence that is in their hands. Who can tell if God will turn and repent, and turn away from His fierce anger, that we perish not? And God Saw their works, that they turned from their evil way; and God Repented of the evil, that He had Said that He would Do unto them; and He Did it not ”.

CONCLUSION

When a person is made prepared for a Storm, yes, there is now an expectation of what should be endured, but it still leaves the unforgivable damages of which it must spark within the mind of what could have been done differently to lessen or to prevent the type of destruction that will now be experienced. Feeding of one thing or one system or of spirits and gods without the breaking of that feeding to cleanse from that feeding will always manifest itself in such items to give birth to that which will and must become an Abomination to The True God that has Established Rules, Standards and Spiritual Guidelines to follow. I've learnt while growing up that half of a bread is much better than no bread, even though the opportunity is there to receive the whole bread, but even though the opportunity is given to receive the complete bread, one must always be careful of the spirits that are feeding, that have activated within a person's vessel to achieve the whole bread at any consequences necessary just to fulfill the need of feeding a spirit of Greed. The spirits of Greed never see The Higher Level nor can it observe to understand The Final View of every path that is now taken to walk upon. Even if feeding causes death to the vessel that is activated to feed, the spirits are 100% what it is, just being made to feed to then move on to the other available vessel to continue to be fed.

It's always a good thing to look at what is available and what is Given by God to take care of, that which is Given by God to enjoy and build; if it is not taken care of or appreciated by mankind then it stands in the possibility of being taken completely away from The Father Above. The Truth about this Book Called GOD'S UGLY is to become A Spiritual Compass for All. A Red Light to say to especially the generation which is to come to manifest The Spiritual Words that says: STOP! YOU ARE GOING TO BE IN DANGER OF GOD'S WRATH! I Hope and Pray that this Book with the Messages thereof will not fall on deaf ears, but there is always the desire within mankind to find out for themselves, even if they have been warned of a thing, they would still need to see for themselves if it is actually the Truth. It happened to Adam and Eve, it took place in the life of Pharaoh and Nebuchadnezzar, therefore, it is observed that the Past has manifested damnation for it self, The Present is hungry to find out if it will happen again, if it's The Same God of the Past that is still Ruling Now and will always be Ruling for All Future events. The Future, if it is not trained by The Past and The Present, will always be looking at a dark hole without the resurrection of climbing out to find the light again. I Acknowledge to my readers that All Glory, Honor and Praise be Offered Always to The Invisible and Visible God, through The Access Name of Jesus Christ, Amen. From The Ministry of The Church of Jesus Christ Fellowship, Savannah Cross, Jamaica, West Indies. From Your Brother, A Minister, A Friend in The Vessel of Being A Servant to God, Pastor Lerone Dinnall. Remain Spiritually Covered, Amen.

www.ingramcontent.com/pod-product-compliance
Lightning Source LLC
Chambersburg PA
CBHW051522120626
46551CB00012B/1033